Making A Comeback

Reclaiming Our Lives in Christ

by

Jeffrey A. Johnson, Sr.

Making A Comeback
by Jeffrey A. Johnson, Sr.

Printed in the United States of America

ISBN 978-1-60647-665-9

www.xulonpress.com

To Audra,

Be Blessed!

To my beloved mentor and friend,

Dr. A. Louis Patterson, Jr.

the man who taught me through expression
and example
what it means to have a pastor's heart
and to be a serious student of scripture

Table of Contents

Foreword

I will never forget the day I went to see my son Jonathan play one of his final games as the starting fullback for Baylor University. Baylor was playing Texas A & M and was losing in the fourth quarter. Baylor put together a drive that scored in the final seconds sending the game into overtime. After three overtimes Baylor threw a touchdown pass that won the game. The crowd by the thousands poured onto the field to celebrate the come-from-behind victory. The goalposts were torn down and later cut up into small pieces and sold as mementos of the great comeback.

Everybody loves a comeback. There is nothing more exciting than to see an athlete or a team that appears to be beaten come back, overcoming the odds, and transforming certain defeat into a glorious victory. This is especially true if it's your favorite athlete or team. In athletics the reward for a come-back is given in terms of money, position and noto-riety. In life the stakes are much, much higher.

This very powerful and practical work by my great friend, Jeffrey Johnson, shows how God can enable each of us to "make a comeback" in our life. It's good news to know that our past does not have to define our future and that our tomorrows can be better than our yesterdays, no matter how ugly things have been.

In *Making A Comeback*, Pastor Johnson reminds us of a God who is able to turn messes into miracles and even incorporate our mistakes, sins and failures into our comebacks. Pastor Johnson has been uniquely gifted to proclaim biblical truth in such a way that it both informs the mind and nourishes the soul, replacing the dark night of despair with the glorious Sonshine of hope.

In this masterfully written work, we have been given a guide for our own personal comeback. Whether it's physical, financial, circumstantial, relational or spiritual, *Making A Comeback* will show you that your story is not over yet. There are chapters for our lives that are yet to be written. If we will simply get in line with God's program and plan, we will see that we are indeed more than conquerors in Christ.

After reading this book I assure you your hopes and dreams of victory and a better tomorrow, that may have long faded, will be renewed and revived. You will dare to believe that what happened in the biblical text can also happen to you. You will discover that the God who gave people back their lives yesterday can give you your life back today.

As you experience the spiritually transforming truths of this book leap off the page and embed themselves into your heart and life, you will have your own testimony of how God can take what looks like a sure defeat and turn it into an awesome victory. And when He gives you your comeback, make sure you don't forget to give Him the praise for turning your life around. After reading this book, you will realize that your comeback is just around the corner.

Dr. Tony Evans
Senior Pastor, Oak Cliff Bible Fellowship
President and Founder,
The Urban Alternative

Introduction

When we become Christians, a lot of wonderful things happen. Old things pass away, and all things become new. We are forgiven. We have the Spirit of Christ dwelling in us. Our consciences are clean. We have a new way of looking at things. Life is sweet. But also in that moment, the enemy of our soul goes into an attack mode. Jesus tells us in John 10:10 that the thief, the enemy, has come "to steal and kill and destroy." Many of us, robbed and separated from God, are now living self-destructive lives because we have been victimized by the enemy of our souls. But the Bible gives us so much hope by reminding us of the fact that God is able to restore everything the enemy has taken from us. We *can* make a comeback. We are not defeated beyond hope. Throughout this book, we will explore selected passages of scripture that will enlighten us and help us in *Making A Comeback* through the power of God's Holy Spirit. Let's look at a quick preview of what is to come:

I. "I Want My Life Back"

When the Bible speaks of death, it speaks in terms of separation. James 2:26 says physical death happens when the body is separated from the spirit. Spiritual death, on the other hand, occurs when a person is separated from a proper relationship with God through His Son Jesus Christ. Eternal death results when a soul is separated eternally in hell from the saving grace of God. In John 11, the way Jesus deals with Lazarus reveals His power to resurrect and restore. God can handle any "dead" predicament. No matter how dead a situation appears, it is not too late for Jesus to step in and bring life. All things are possible with God, even when they seem impossible to us.

II. "I Want My Health Back"

In 2 Kings 5:14, God proves He is Jehovah Rapha, the God who heals. Faith does impact fitness. Naaman had leprosy, which affected him biologically, psychologically, emotionally, and socially. Yet faith in the plan of God brought deliverance to his situation. Throughout scripture, God manifests His ability to heal any sickness. As we put our confidence in God, He releases His anointing to heal.

III. "I Want My Mind Back"

There are battles and unrest in Iraq, Afghanistan, other areas of the Middle East, various regions of Africa, and throughout the world. But the greatest war being waged is the battle for the mind. The mind is a battlefield where the enemy attempts to get his greatest victory. As we look at our own decisions, choices, and behavior, it appears that some of us have lost our minds. Thank God, that through Jesus and His Holy Spirit, He has equipped us to get the victory over our minds, thus enabling us to get the victory in our lives as well. In this chapter, we will study the principles necessary to reclaim our minds.

IV. "I Want My Stuff Back"

Similar to David in 1 Samuel 29 and 30, so many of us have lost money, houses, friends, influence, jobs, spouses, and children. Here in His Word, God demonstrates to us that, working through us, He can restore everything that we have lost. David's experience teaches us the reasons for our loss, as well as actions we can take to regain what was lost. We can get our stuff back.

V. "I Want My Family Back"

In Genesis 14, Abraham's life experience reflects what is true in many of our lives—we have relatives who are in bondage. Far too often we find our own relatives enslaved to drugs, alcohol, or a host of other things that keep them from living the life they were intended to live. The story of Abraham shows us the steps he took to free his relatives and win them back. As we look at these principles and practices, we can gain the knowledge to get our own families back.

VI. *"I Want My Groove Back"*

The apostle Paul writes in 1 Corinthians about the fact that there are people who have lost their groove. Maybe he doesn't use that term exactly, but he lets us know that both singles and married couples have major issues at times with relationships. The groove is gone. The joy and happiness they once experienced in those relationships are now absent. The willingness to compromise and openly communicate is lost. Even commitment and fidelity to each other are gone. Yet Paul, inspired by God's Holy Spirit, reveals how we might get our groove back in our relationships. And note that it's "groove," not "rut"! For some, the Word of God says to go back and get what we have lost. For others of us, it means moving forward to take hold of new possibilities that God makes available so that we can get our groove back.

VII. *"I Want My Joy Back"*

King David had position, possessions, palaces, prestige, prominence, and much more, but what he did not have was joy. His life shows us that, in spite of all that we may have, our attitudes and actions can rob us of our joy. Many of us have not lost our salvation, but we have lost the joy that comes with our salvation. There is something we can do, however, to regain our joy. It is time for us to embrace the principle that God's Word provides for us to get our joy back.

VIII. The Greatest Comeback Ever

Jesus had died and was buried. This Person that many believed to be the Messiah was gone. The One that many thought was going to set up a kingdom of which they could be a part was now lying dead in a tomb. The Teacher whom the disciples had left everything to follow was no longer there to lead them. Life, as those Christ-followers had known it, was over. Sad, afraid, and not even able to comprehend what the death of Jesus meant, the disciples sat in a locked room and did nothing. But Jesus didn't stay in the tomb! Jesus made the greatest comeback ever when God raised Him from the dead on the third day. That same God is still able to raise our "dead" situations. Even when all looks lost, God is able to empower us to make a comeback.

As you read through each chapter of this book, I am trusting God to help you learn how to make your own comeback. Whatever your area of need, regardless how hopeless it looks, the same Spirit that raised Christ from the dead also dwells in you. (See Romans

8:11.) Jesus has come so that we "might have life and have it more abundantly" (John 10:10). Let this book become your personal guide to making a comeback.

I

I Want My Life Back

³⁸Jesus, once more deeply moved, came to the tomb. It was a cave with a stone laid across the entrance. ³⁹"Take away the stone," he said. "But, Lord," said Martha, the sister of the dead man, "by this time there is a bad odor, for he has been there four days."

⁴⁰Then Jesus said, "Did I not tell you that if you believed, you would see the glory of God?" ⁴¹So they took away the stone. Then Jesus looked up and said, "Father, I thank you that you have heard me. ⁴²I knew that you always hear me, but I said this for the benefit of the people standing here, that they may believe that you sent me."

⁴³When he had said this, Jesus called in a loud voice, "Lazarus, come out!" ⁴⁴The dead man came out, his hands and feet wrapped with strips of linen, and a cloth around his face.

Jesus said to them, "Take off the grave clothes and let him go."

(John 11:38-44)

In Phenix City, Alabama, one of the business leaders of the community was a car dealer, and everybody knew that he had money. One night his twelve-year-old son was at the car dealership with him. All the customers and other employees had left. Some thieves came in and stole the man's money from him; then, they took him and his young son to a wooded area. There they killed the twelve-year-old boy and cut the throat of the father. Afterward, they put the man in a shallow grave and left him for dead, thinking they had gotten away with this robbery and murder.

But somehow, even after being ripped off, even after suffering the loss of a family member, and even after being left for dead with his throat cut, this man was able to dig himself out of the shallow grave. He went to the nearest house, and the people there called the authorities, who caught his assailants. The man went to the hospital and got the medical attention he needed; and the assailants went to prison.

I'm telling this story because some of you reading this book may have had to deal with cutthroats. The enemy has attacked you. You used to have something, but the enemy has taken it away from you. Even a family member you used to have, you don't have anymore. But I'm writing this chapter to tell you that if this man could dig his way out of everything the enemy did to him physically, you can dig your way out spiritually. No matter how hard it's been, no matter how difficult, no matter what the cutthroat did to you, I believe you can dig your way out. No matter what you've been buried in, it is possible to get your life back.

Everyone Suffers

This message of hope that I'm bringing to you is set against the backdrop of the Gospel of John, chapter 11. Verse 1 tells us that the setting for John's story is in Bethany, which is just a few miles outside of Jerusalem. Martha, her sister Mary, and her brother Lazarus lived there. They loved Jesus so much that anytime you read about them in the scriptures, they are opening their hearts and their home to Jesus. He would often stay with them. Even when Jesus was preaching in Jerusalem, He would not stay in the Jerusalem Hilton Inn, but He would stay at the house of Martha, Mary, and Lazarus. Mary would sit at the feet of Jesus and listen as He taught in their home. Mary worshiped and celebrated Jesus, the Christ. Mary was such a worshiper, in fact, that she once broke open a bottle of expensive perfume and anointed Jesus' feet with it. Mary was such a worshiper that when she worshiped Jesus, she did so openly and extravagantly. She was willing to praise God even against the protest of other people, even when they didn't understand what she knew—that Jesus is worthy to be praised, worshiped, and honored.

But wait a minute. It wasn't just Mary who loved Jesus. At this house in Bethany, Mary's sister Martha also loved Him. She would care for Jesus, making sure He had a comfortable place to stay and good food to eat. Undoubtedly, she would even serve Him His favorite meals; and not only would she serve Jesus, but also anyone else He brought into the house with Him. This was a wonderful family.

In this family, there was also a brother named Lazarus, who was a witness for Jesus. Now, as a student of the Bible, you may point out to me that nowhere in the Bible do we see any mention of Lazarus witnessing. In fact, he is not recorded as saying anything at all. Then, you ask, "How are you going to call him a witness when he's not recorded as saying anything?" That's because he didn't have to witness verbally; he was witnessing visibly. People could look at him and see the power of God. In this portion of scripture, Lazarus died, but Jesus raised him from the dead. So every time people saw Lazarus, they saw someone who had experienced the power of God in his life. As a matter of fact, it says in the next chapter that when people came to Jerusalem and to nearby Bethany looking for Jesus, they wanted to see Jesus *and* Lazarus. They wanted to see Jesus because He could *raise* the dead, and they wanted to see Lazarus because he'd been raised *from* the dead.

As my mentor, Dr. A. Louis Patterson, Jr., points out, that's how it ought to be with those of us who are Christians. When folk come to church looking for Jesus, they should want to see us too, because we were dead in sin but God raised us up. They ought to see at least two things: 1) a Savior who saves sinners; and 2) a sinner who's been saved. Now, the Savior who saves sinners is Jesus, but the sinners who've been saved are us. We ought to be witnesses for Him.

Notice that Martha, Mary, and Lazarus opened up their home. They also opened up their hearts by sharing, serving, supporting, and witnessing for Jesus. That's what we ought to do. Yet, even after opening their hearts and home to Jesus, pain still came into their situation. Verse 3 says that Lazarus became very sick. Despite the fact that this family loved and served Jesus, sickness still came into their home.

In our day, there is a lot of false teaching going around. One doctrine teaches that if you love Jesus and open your heart to Him, no harm is going to come your way. That's why it's so important that we read the Bible for ourselves. Here's a family that opened up their whole hearts to the Lord, and pain still came. Suffering still came. When you become a Christian, you do not become immune to suffering. God has one Son who knew no sin, but God hasn't had any children who have known no suffering. Even Jesus was spit upon. Even Jesus was lied to, laughed at, had His hands nailed to a cross, and had a spike pounded into His feet. Jesus Himself warned us: "Now if you see they will do this to a 'green tree,' to someone who has never sinned, never made a mistake, never messed up—somebody who came straight from God—what makes you think they won't do it to an old, dried up, withered tree (to someone who is guilty)?" (See Luke 23:31.) No matter how much you love and serve God, you will have tribulation!

But for some of you, people are telling you that your suffering is because of sin. Now, anytime you sin, you *will* suffer, but you can also suffer without sinning. You can mind your own business, and trouble will still come your way. Some people will tell you the reason you're going through problems on your job is because of a lack of faith; the reason you've got sickness in your home is because of your lack of faith; the reason your house got foreclosed on is because of your lack of faith; and the reason your family fell apart is because of your lack of faith. Isn't it interesting that when these misfortunes happen to *you*, it's because of a lack of faith; but when they happen to *them*, it's an attack of the devil? Just because you've opened your heart to Jesus doesn't mean pain isn't going to come your way.

Delayed Response

But look at what we learn from Martha and Mary when their brother Lazarus got sick. Verse 3 says they sent word to Jesus. (I love this. Just because trouble comes our way doesn't mean we stop talking to Jesus.) Martha and Mary sent word to Jesus: "Lord, the one you love is sick," or, in the King James Version, "Lord, behold, he whom thou lovest is sick." Their message to Jesus was, "The one you *phileo*—love as a brother, love as a friend—is sick." Those present when Jesus got the message must have stood back, resting assured that Jesus was going to immediately run right to this house. After all, here was a family who served Him, gave to Him, offered Him shelter, and loved Him. Just to be sure that we knew how Jesus felt about this family, John 11: 5 says plainly, "Jesus loved Martha and her sister and Lazarus." Surely, when sickness came to this house, Jesus was going to show up in a hurry.

But Jesus didn't hurry; instead, He took His time. Contrary to what everyone expected, He waited two more days before setting off for Bethany. So by the time Jesus got there, Lazarus was not merely sick: he had died. He had even been in the tomb for four days. So when Jesus finally showed up after such a long delay, Martha and Mary had an attitude with Him. Because He delayed coming, Lazarus had already gone from a sick situation to a dead situation, to a grave situation, and now was in a stinking situation. So both sisters, in turn, walked up to Jesus and said, "Jesus, if You had been here, my brother would not have died." They were actually telling Him, "If You had been here, things would be different. If You had come when we called You, we wouldn't be mourning like this. If You had come when we asked You to come, everything would have been all right."

Now, let's not pretend that we've never had an attitude with Jesus. Most of us would have been thinking the same thing: "Jesus, You've helped people who didn't even know You. You've healed people who didn't even ask to be healed. You have worked in the lives of other folk who didn't even have any knowledge of You. But here we are. We've served You, cooked for You, and even opened up our home to You. Then *we* call on *You*, and You don't show up. Other folk don't even call for You, and yet You bless *them*."

Let's bring it closer to home. Your coworker never goes to church. You wonder how it is that person is getting a promotion while you're at church every time the door opens and yet nothing's happening in your career. Okay, you've never had an attitude with Jesus? Every Sunday, your neighbors are out washing their cars to get ready to go play golf, while you're getting ready to go to church to worship God, hear the Word, and give your tithe to the Lord. Yet their property is bigger, their house is nicer, and their family is getting along better. You're trying to figure out why God is showing up over there when they don't even serve Him, but you're trying to please Him and nothing is happening. Okay, you've never had an attitude with Jesus? While you're standing outside in the cold at the bus stop with your bus pass in hand, here comes a drug dealer driving by in his Benz. You're trying to figure this thing out: "Lord, if You'd do what I've asked You to do, it wouldn't be like this."

Look even more closely at how Jesus loved this family. Remember that verse 3 tells us Jesus loved (*phileo*, "brotherly love") Lazarus. But verse 5 is even stronger. It tells us Jesus loved (*agape*, "unconditional love") Martha, Mary, and Lazarus. He loved them unconditionally. He loved them "in spite of," and yet trouble still came to them. You say, "That's the problem! How can Jesus love me, but not use His power to help me?" You've never thought that? Maybe these thoughts sounds familiar: He's supposed to have all power and be able to do all things, but I've been calling on Him for three years about my health, and I'm still not healed. I've been praying to Him for six months about my job, and still nothing else has opened up. I've been praying to Him about my family; but it still fell apart, and now I'm losing my mind. He's supposed to have all power, and He's supposed to love me, but if He loved me, you'd think He'd use His power to help me. Maybe He loves me, but He just doesn't have the power to change my situation. Or, maybe He has the power to change my situation, but He just doesn't love me.

Let me help you understand something. Anytime you question the love of God, look at Calvary. Look at the Cross. God so loved the world (including us) that He gave His Son, Jesus. "God demonstrates his own love for us in this: While we were yet sinners, Christ died for us" (Romans 5:8). He didn't wait until we got better. While we were still sinners, He gave His Son for us. Christ died for us. When you think that God doesn't love you, look at Calvary. Calvary screams the love of God in your life.

"Well," you say, "maybe He loves me, but He doesn't have the power to change my situation." When you question God's power, don't just look at Calvary; look at the resurrection. The resurrection speaks of the power of God. Even though Jesus died on Friday, three days later, God raised Him from the dead. Jesus stood on resurrection ground and said that not just some power, but "ALL power is in My hand." Wait a minute, you say, help me to understand this: God loves me, and He has power; but my situation hasn't changed. I don't understand that.

Don't Give Up!

Let me clear it up for you. Yes, God loves you, and yes, He has the power to change your situation. But God can do whatever He wants to do, whenever He gets ready to do it. He can use whomever He pleases, and He can do it without input from you or me because He's *sovereign*. God is God. He created us; we did not create Him. Perhaps, therefore, He knows best. Just maybe the One who created the sun, the earth and all of the universe has a better vantage point than we have; maybe what looks "right" in our eyes, looks different from where He is sitting.

Here's something I love about Martha. Even though she was in trouble, she still trusted Jesus: "If You had come when we called You, I know things would have been different. My brother would not have died. But I know that even now…." Do you hear her trust in Jesus? In essence, she says, "We've got trouble. I don't know why You didn't come when we called, but I still trust You. I believe that You are the Christ that has come into the world; I know that even now…" What I'm trying to tell you is that even when you can't trace Jesus, you've got to keep on trusting Jesus. When you cannot trace His hand, you've got to keep on trusting His heart because the timing of God is at work in this situation. You've got to understand that just because He has delayed doesn't mean He has denied your request. Just because God didn't come when you called Him doesn't mean He isn't coming at all. Just because Martha called but Jesus didn't come till four days later doesn't mean He denied her prayer. He just delayed answering that prayer.

You may be praying right now to God for something major, either in your life or that of a loved one. You've been fasting, you've been trusting, and you're wondering, "Where is God?" Receive what I'm saying. Just because He's delayed His coming doesn't mean He's denied your request. He will come. My grandma said, "He may not come when you want Him. He's a God you can't hurry. He may not come when you want Him, but He's always right on time." He's an on-time God.

You see, here's the situation. There are no emergencies with God. The message came: "Jesus, the one that You love is sick." But He took two days before He even left. When He came moseying into town, Martha went out to meet Him: "Jesus, if You had been here, my brother would not have died." Jesus could well have told her, "There are no emergencies with Me."

God doesn't get in a hurry over things that upset you. Do you really think that God is up in glory, pacing the streets of gold, wondering how He's going to get you out of this mess? Do you hear Him worrying, "Well, they've really gotten themselves in a mess this time." Do you see God wringing His hands, saying, "I wonder what I should do? I just don't know how I'm going to help them out this time!" No, friend, there are no emergencies with God.

Jesus' disciples, the twelve who traveled with Him, had to learn that lesson. They were on a boat one day when a storm arose suddenly. With the wind, the rain, and the waves, their boat was rapidly filling up with water. With their buckets, they were frantically trying to bail water out, while at the same time trying to steady the boat to keep it from capsizing. In the midst of that chaos, they looked around and discovered someone who wasn't helping or working. Peter was there. Matthew was there. All of the other disciples were there, but Jesus wasn't there. Guess where Jesus was. He was in the back part of the ship, asleep! I repeat: there are no emergencies with Jesus.

Here's what's especially telling about the situation. Dr. Patterson points out that Mark 4:38 tells us Jesus was asleep on a pillow. That means that Jesus didn't just *fall* asleep. He went and got a pillow and in the midst of their crisis, He went to sleep. Here, they're working, struggling and crying, "Jesus, where are You? You don't care. Don't You care that we live or die?" And here He is, lying on a bed of blessings, wrapped in a cover of comfort, with His head on a pillow of peace. But when He finally rose up in that situation and wiped the sleep out of His eyes, He said, "Peace! Be still!" The storm ceased, the waves became calm, and the disaster was over. Whenever He shows up, things will get better. There are no emergencies with Him, but you're trying to hurry God in your situation. You're trying to *rush* Him.

Dr. James Jackson, pastor of New Beginnings Fellowship Church in Indianapolis, tells of a woman who killed two of her three children and then committed suicide. An older child escaped and ran for help. Everyone asked how a mother could possibly do that. What would cause a woman to take the lives of her own children? The grandmother of the children, in the midst of her shock and pain, was interviewed by reporters. She explained that her daughter obviously had a number of issues, but what put her over the edge and caused her to do such a terrible thing was that she could not afford to buy her children any school clothes. She let it eat at her. She felt like less of a mother, less of a woman, because she couldn't provide school clothes for her children like the other parents were buying for their children. That was the final blow to her fragile self-image, and she couldn't face the idea of failing her children yet again. So, in her sick state of mind, she killed her children and herself. The anguished grandmother went on to say that what was especially tragic was that: "I had already gone to the store, and had bought new clothes for all the kids, and had put the clothes in their closet to surprise them." Now, here all these clothes had already been purchased and stored for them; what they needed was already available to them. The grandmother was just waiting to surprise them. But the mother got so distraught that she took her own life before she went into the closet and got her surprise.

You ask, "Why are you telling us this?" Because someone reading this book is distressed, dismayed, and disillusioned. You're upset with God and distraught with the world because you don't understand that you've got a secret closet. If you go into this secret closet and pray to God privately, He will reward you openly. You've got to learn to wait on God. You may be ready to give up. You are physically and emotionally tired, thinking all your hope is in vain. You would do almost anything to get rid of the pain you feel right now — to stop those voices in your head that are mocking you. But you have to remember that God is an on-time God. Yes, He is! He may not come when you want Him, but He'll be there right on time. Don't give up now; the answer to your situation is already in the works.

Jesus Will Show Up

Now watch these same attitudes of impatience and lack of understanding at work within the disciples when Jesus got the message about Lazarus. While Jesus was waiting, they were worrying. After two days, the disciples were saying, "Jesus, don't we need to hurry up and get to Bethany so that You can heal Lazarus?" Jesus said, "Lazarus is asleep." "Oh, okay," the disciples responded, "if he's asleep, then he's doing well." Jesus explained, "You misunderstand what I'm telling you. Lazarus is dead." Then Jesus said this: "And I'm glad I wasn't there." What?! Jesus' friend Lazarus got sick and died, and Jesus—the Savior, the Healer, the Compassionate One—said, "And I'm glad I wasn't there." That sounds horribly insensitive, doesn't it?

But we have a High Priest who understands and identifies with what we are going through. When Jesus said, "I'm glad I wasn't there," it was not because He was insensitive to the pain and suffering of Mary and Martha, or even of Lazarus, who probably died thinking that Jesus would be coming any second and all would be well. What Jesus was saying is, "I'm glad I wasn't there because had I been there, they would not be able to see what they're getting ready to see. Had I shown up when they wanted Me to show up, they would not be able to experience the glory of God in the way they're going to experience it now. Had I shown up when they thought I should have been there, they would not have been able to be blessed by the miracle that they are going to experience. I'm glad I was not there."

That's the word Jesus may have for you. You called on Him four years ago, and He didn't show up. You got upset, but Jesus said, "I'm glad I wasn't there." "I'm glad I wasn't there when that man walked out, because you had so much trust in him, and he wasn't worthy of your trust. But now you've learned how to trust in Me, and now you have a much better image of yourself than when he was with you, putting you down. I'm glad I wasn't there!" "When they laid you off from that job, I wanted you to be someplace better anyway, or to start your own business. That was a dead-end job that made you feel bad about yourself; you needed something better. I'm glad I wasn't there!"

Here's the thing. Someone reading this book is mad at Jesus, saying, "How can He let me go through all of this?" But Jesus is saying to that person, "I'm glad I wasn't there, because had you not gone through some of the stuff you've gone through, you would not be the kind of person you are right now." You see, it's the struggle that builds strength. It's the crisis that gives you character. Had Jesus shown up when we thought He should have, we would not be the kind of people we are today.

My friend Dr. Theron Williams, pastor of Mt. Carmel Baptist Church in Indianapolis, tells the story about this little bird that lived in Indiana. Of course, it gets cold in Indiana, so the birds fly south to Florida for the winter. But this bird procrastinated and took his time leaving to fly south. The early birds had gone first, and then the others had all left; but this was the last bird remaining in Indiana. It was saying, "I'll get there when I get there." But he was still around when the temperature began to drop suddenly into the single-digits and then fell to below-zero. Now the bird was sitting on a barren tree branch, freezing to death. His wings got so cold they froze, and he fell out of the tree to the ground, no longer able to fly. There he was, lying frozen on the ground, thinking to himself, "I don't know why I was procrastinating. I should have gotten out of here a long time ago." He resigned himself to the fact that he was going to freeze to death because of his own procrastination.

Then along comes a horse that needed to relieve himself, just at the moment he was standing over the frozen bird. So here was the bird in the midst of all of this fresh manure, mad at God. He was really angry and complaining, "God, I know I should have flown south for the winter. I know You gave me time. I know I should have gotten out of here a long time ago. I know it's my fault that I froze. But, God, out of all the places this horse could have relieved himself, it didn't have to be here. You could have had him do it a few inches away. Instead, You let this horse put me in all this manure." But while the bird was complaining in the midst of all of this mess, the manure began to melt the ice and warm up his wings so that they were no longer frozen. Soon he was able to fly and move on to his destination. Here's what I'm trying to tell you. Stop crying and complaining in the midst of your mess! God is going to use that mess to thaw out your frozen situation and get you to your destination.

I want you to see the restoration process in this. I want you to see that you can get your life back. I want you to see that no matter how dead your situation looks, it isn't over. You've gone from bad to worse, and it looks hopeless right now. You've been praying to God, and He hasn't shown up the way that you think He should. I want you to know that you're getting ready to see the glory of God in your situation, if you just believe.

Here in Bethany, Jesus showed up, and Mary and Martha said the same thing: "If You had been here, my brother would not have died. I believe that even now, whatever You ask God for, God will do it." Jesus told them, "Your brother is going to rise again; he's going to live again." "Well, I know he's going to rise again in the last day." "I'm not talking about the last day. I'm talking about the One who is standing in front of you right now. I AM the resurrection and the life." So here are Jesus and Martha going back and forth. Jesus says, "Go get Mary from the house." Mary came, and she started getting upset, so Jesus said to her, "Listen, just show Me where you laid him." So they went to the tomb.

It was a cave with a stone rolled in front of it. When they get there, Jesus said, "Now roll the stone away." Martha started protesting, "But, Jesus, by now he stinks. He's been in there four days." In essence, Jesus said, "I didn't ask you about the condition. I asked you to show Me the location. Show Me where you laid him. Show Me where you walked away from the situation. Show Me where you thought I was too late. Show Me where you didn't think I could do anything. Show Me where you gave up. Show Me where you threw in the towel. Show Me where you held up the white flag of surrender. Show Me where you got ready to turn your back on God. Show Me where you thought I was too late. Roll the stone away!"

Believing is Seeing

Jesus says to you as He did to Mary and Martha, "Didn't I tell you if you just believe that you would see the glory of God?" I know it's hard. I know it's difficult. I know it seems impossible. Here's the problem. Too many people think, "Well, if God shows me His glory, *then* I will believe." God says, "No, you've got to believe it, *then* I will show you My glory." I'm trying to show you the glory of God in this text. I'm trying to show you how Lazarus got his stuff restored, because if you want your life back, it is possible for you to get it back.

They rolled the stone away, and then the text says, "Jesus looked up." I wonder in which direction you've been looking. Looking down at others? Looking at your problem? Looking at your issue? Looking at your hard times? Jesus said that if you want it back, you've got to change the direction you look. You've got to look up to God. You've got to look up to the hills from where your help comes. Do you know your help comes from the Lord? Jesus looked up, and then He said, "Father." Is it possible that you have forgotten the relationship you have with God? Is it possible that you've been spending so much time analyzing God and your situation that you've forgotten about the relationship? You see, His ways are not our ways. His thoughts are not our thoughts. They are higher than our thoughts, even as the heavens are high above the earth. So instead of focusing on God whom I don't always understand, I'm going to focus on the fact that I still am in a relationship with Him.

The scripture tells us that Jesus wept. Yet in the midst of His tears, He still recognized God as His Father. Here's what I'm trying to tell you: even when you don't understand *God*, you've still got to trust Him as *Father*. When Jesus was dying on the cross, the people had whipped Him, beat Him, pounded nails into His hands, put spikes into His feet, lied about Him, and falsely accused Him. He was dying an excruciatingly painful death. One of the seven last sayings of Jesus was, "Eli, Eli, lama sabachthani?" which means, "My God, my God, why have You forsaken me?" So, even Jesus had some questions for God. But before it was over, He said, "*Father*, into Your hands, I commend My spirit." "My *God*, My *God*, why?" "My *Father*, into Your hands I commend My spirit." *God*, why? *Father*, I give it all to You.

You see, there are times when I don't understand everything about God. I don't know why He hasn't shown up. I don't know why He hasn't moved. I don't know why He hasn't raised what has died in my situation. I question *God*, but I still trust in Him as my *Father*, and I put my situation into His hands.

When Jesus was standing before the tomb where Lazarus was buried, and all the people were gathered around, He said, "Father, I thank You...." (He was still thanking Him in the midst of the trouble.) "I thank You that you've already heard Me." Dr. Patterson says that now we know why Jesus took two days before He left—because He spent those two days in prayer. That's why He didn't *start* praying when He first got there. Instead, He said, "Father, I know that you have *already* heard Me. I have already talked with You about this, and the only reason I'm praying now is because I want these folk around here to benefit by believing."

It's not enough to call on God, and then not have confidence in the One you call on. You've already prayed about your situation. You've already called upon Him. Now have confidence that God *heard* you. Okay, maybe this is your problem: you say, "I called on Him, and I'm trying to believe He heard, but why hasn't He shown up yet?" Let me explain the time element in this account. Jesus delayed for two days before starting out in response to the message that Lazarus was sick. By the time He got there, Lazarus had been dead four days. That's precisely why it took Jesus that long to get there. He wanted to make sure Lazarus had been dead for at least four days. You see, the Hebrew people in the first century believed that the spirit or soul of a person who died would hover around the body for three days, trying to get back into the body. But on the fourth day, the soul would go where it was supposed to go. So Jesus was saying, in effect, "If I had come any sooner, people could explain away the miracle."

A Greater Miracle

It is recorded three times in the Bible that Jesus raised somebody from the dead. Jesus raised Jairus' twelve-year-old daughter, but she had died just before Jesus got to the house. Jesus came in and said, "Little girl, get up," and He raised her from the dead. But somebody may argue she really wasn't dead; she just fainted.

The next time, it was the widow's son in Nain. His body was actually being carried in the funeral procession on the way to the graveyard when Jesus spotted the young man's mother and had compassion on her. The Hebrew people of that time would bury those who died the next day, so this man had scarcely been dead for twenty-four hours when Jesus touched his coffin and he got up. Since it was still within that three-day period, somebody might have said, "The young man wasn't really dead; he just swooned." So Jesus may have thought, "All right. You're saying the little girl fainted and the young man swooned, so if I show up to raise Lazarus within the three days, somebody's going to say, 'Lazarus wasn't dead; he was just in a coma.'"

So Jesus waited two more days before He started His journey. When He showed up, Martha said of her brother, "He's been dead now four days." Jesus thought, "This is just what I've been looking for." He said to the people, "Now roll the stone away." Then

He called out, "Lazarus, come forth!" I like the way the old preacher says that Jesus had to call him forth by name, because if He had just said, "Come forth," Abraham would have gotten up, Isaac would have gotten up, Jacob would have gotten up; every person who had died would have gotten up. He had to call the dead man by his name. And Jesus, in your dead situation, knows *your* name. That's why the old folk used to sing, "Hush! Hush! Somebody's calling my name.... Sounds like Jesus."

When Jesus raised that little girl from the dead, the Sadducees didn't try to kill Him. When Jesus raised the widow's son from the dead, they didn't try to kill Him. But when He raised Lazarus from the dead after four days, the Sadducees tried to kill Him because they didn't believe in the resurrection of the dead. Now Jesus had contradicted their theology. They didn't believe in the resurrection of the dead, and yet everybody is coming from all over the place to see Jesus and Lazarus, whom He raised from the dead. They would rather kill Lazarus than to rethink their theology.

There may be some people right now who are trying to kill you. You're trying to be a Christian; you're trying to be right, to be filled with the Holy Spirit, and to do your thing for God, and there are folk trying to destroy your character, even lying about you. You're puzzled, trying to figure out why. It's because you're messing with their theology. They believe, "If you don't go to my church, if you're not in my denomination, if you don't submit to my bishop, then your stuff isn't real." And here you are, walking around filled with the Holy Spirit and experiencing a great change in your life, so your very life is challenging their theology. They would rather kill you than to consider that, like the wind, the Spirit blows where He pleases and you hear the sound of Him, but you don't know where He's coming from or where He's going. If your life disproves their beliefs, it is easier in their minds to "kill" you than to rethink their theology.

Let me finish this chapter the way I started. I told you at the beginning about the man who owned the car dealership. Thieves broke into his dealership, stole from him, and took him and his son into the woods. After killing his son, they cut the man's throat and threw him in a shallow grave, but he was able to dig his way out and go find help. I told one of my pastor friends that story, but I found out later that he didn't believe me at the time. He thought I had gotten my facts wrong. He told me a few months later, "I just couldn't believe it, because when you cut somebody's throat, it bleeds very fast and they die quickly. So I didn't believe it until I saw it on the Internet." I said, "Wait a minute. You've known me for twenty years, and you didn't believe me. You don't know who put that story on the Internet, but you believed *them*?" He said, "No, you didn't tell the whole story." "What are you talking about?" I asked. He said, "What you didn't tell me was that when they threw him in the shallow grave, the dirt they threw on him got into the cut on his neck. That dirt is what kept him from bleeding to death. So, what his enemies were using to try to destroy him, God was using to deliver him."

I want you to know that while your enemies are trying to destroy you, even though they mean it for evil, God is going to use it for your good. Don't worry about what it looks like at the moment. God knows what He's doing. He knows the best time to come on the scene and bring your miracle. Remember that He loves you in spite of how your circumstances look right now. He loves you in spite of what other people are telling you. He loves you in spite of the doubts that plague your own mind. Keep on trusting. Thank Him for your mountains and for your valleys. Trust Him that He is going to work it all together for your good and for His glory.

II

I Want My Health Back

[1]Now Naaman was commander of the army of the king of Aram. He was a great man in the sight of his master and highly regarded, because through him the Lord had given victory to Aram. He was a valiant soldier, but he had leprosy.

[2]Now bands from Aram had gone out and had taken captive a young girl from Israel, and she served Naaman's wife. [3]She said to her mistress, "If only my master would see the prophet who is in Samaria! He would cure him of his leprosy."

[4]Naaman went to his master and told him what the girl from Israel had said. [5]"By all means, go," the king of Aram replied. "I will send a letter to the king of Israel." So Naaman left, taking with him ten talents of silver, six thousand shekels of gold and ten sets of clothing. [6]The letter that he took to the king of Israel read: "With this letter I am sending my servant Naaman to you so that you may cure him of his leprosy." [7]As soon as the king of Israel read the letter, he tore his robes and said, "Am I God? Can I kill and bring back

to life? Why does this fellow send someone to me to be cured of his leprosy? See how he is trying to pick a quarrel with me!"

[8]When Elisha the man of God heard that the king of Israel had torn his robes, he sent him this message: "Why have you torn your robes? Have the man come to me and he will know that there is a prophet in Israel." [9]So Naaman went with his horses and chariots and stopped at the door of Elisha's house. [10]Elisha sent a messenger to say to him, "Go, wash yourself seven times in the Jordan, and your flesh will be restored and you will be cleansed."

[11]But Naaman went away angry and said, "I thought that he would surely come out to me and stand and call on the name of the Lord his God, wave his hand over the spot and cure me of my leprosy. [12]Are not Abana and Pharpar, the rivers of Damascus, better than any of the waters of Israel? Couldn't I wash in them and be cleansed?" So he turned and went off in a rage.

[13]Naaman's servants went to him and said, "My father, if the prophet had told you to do some great thing, would you not have done it? How much more, then, when he tells you, 'Wash and be cleansed'!" [14]So he went down and dipped himself in the Jordan seven times, as the man of God had told him, and his flesh was restored and became clean like that of a young boy.

(2 Kings 5:1-14)

In Exodus 15:26, God identified Himself to the people of Israel as "the Lord [in Hebrew, *Jehovah*] that heals [in Hebrew, *rapha*] you." In Psalm 103:2-3, David sings praises and blesses this Lord [*Jehovah*] who "forgives all your sins and heals [*rapha*] all your diseases." Elsewhere in the Bible as well we see this identification of God as Jehovah Rapha, the God who heals.

There is an enemy of the people of God. He comes to kill, steal, and destroy. Among the things the enemy comes to try to steal is our health and strength. But I want you to know that no matter how ill you or a member of your family may be, God is still Jehovah Rapha. He is still the God who heals.

With God, All Things Are Possible

I realize that some people today will tell you that because of the dispensation of time that we live in, God is no longer into supernatural healing. They insist that He only performed healing in the Bible days to strengthen the faith and belief of the people, and He doesn't do that anymore. But our God is the same yesterday, today, and forever. If you want to know what somebody is going to do, you can best tell by looking at what they've already done. If you're thinking, "I wonder what this person is going to do in response to this situation; I wonder how she is going to act," look at how she's already acted in the past. When we read about our God in the Bible, we see that He healed many, many people. So, based on what He's already done, we can know what He *will* do. You may even know on a personal level that God heals because He has healed you of something in the past, or He has healed someone you know. We know from experience that God has the power to heal—the power to restore.

Even now, you may want to make a comeback in the area of your physical life; you may be trying to get your health and strength back. Dr. Wayne Dyer, noted counselor, author and speaker, said that if you are looking for an answer but you don't believe it, even if God reveals it to you, you still won't benefit from it because you don't believe it. Dyer also goes so far as to say that if you are looking for an answer, even though things may look bad now, if you truly *believe it*, God will reveal the answer to you. If you are serious about making a comeback, and serious about having your health back and your strength restored, or serious about seeking health and strength for someone you care about, I want you to know that if you believe it, God will reveal to you the answer you need to get the health you are seeking.

But we don't have to take Wayne Dyer's word for it. Jesus said that all things are possible to them that believe. This means that if you don't believe, it is impossible, but if you do believe, God has the power to step into your situation and bring healing. He is Jehovah Rapha. I am writing about this against the backdrop of 2 Kings, chapter 5. This chapter opens with the story of Naaman, a man who was the captain of the Syrian army, a very high and powerful leadership position at that time. According to 2 Kings, the Syrian army appeared to be a world superpower that could go into any nation and defeat any army at any time. And Naaman was the leader of this valiant army. But not only did he hold this prestigious leadership position, but he was also a person who displayed great character and valor. He was courageous and highly regarded by others in his community, even by the king of Syria. He was a man of means; he had great riches. He owned horses, chariots, silver, gold, clothes, and all the things which showed he was a man of means, a man of power and influence, and a man of high position.

More Than Skin Deep

But verse 1 of 2 Kings 5 closes by saying Naaman is a leper. Think about it. He has strength, power, and position. And the verse says that the Lord had used Naaman to help Syria win many military victories. Yet with all of that going for him, he still has a sickness: he has leprosy. Leprosy, an infectious skin disease that was common in that day, was highly contagious because there was no treatment back then. But leprosy had more than just a physical dimension. It *was* a physical disease with skin lesions, sores, crippling, and deformity. But it had an emotional effect on the sufferer as well. The late Dr. E. K. Bailey, founding pastor of Concord Church in Dallas, said that the mind and the body are so closely related they catch each other's diseases. This means that if you stay physically sick long enough, it starts messing with your mind. Conversely, if your mind becomes sick, your physical body can also become ill, if you're not careful.

It wasn't hard for persons who had leprosy in biblical days to have their minds affected, along with their bodies. The disease was so highly contagious that Israel had enacted a law stating lepers could not go out in public where they would have contact with others, not even to the temple. In addition, according to the Israelite law, if persons with leprosy came within fifty feet of someone else, they would have to cry out, "Unclean! Unclean!" In other words, there was a social stigma attached to this sickness.

As you are reading this, you may feel that although you don't have leprosy, you can understand at least a little bit of what someone with leprosy went through. Your own illness may be a physical one, or it may be a mental or psychological disorder, but it has also affected you emotionally and socially. Emotionally, you feel depressed and don't like who you are right now. You feel that you haven't been "normal" in so long, you don't even remember what normal feels like. Your social life has also been affected. You don't hang out with your friends the way you used to. You don't even go to church the way you used to. You don't do the things you used to do for recreation. Why? Because you've been sick. Perhaps it isn't your own decision that you no longer live the life you once lived; maybe it is your friends who avoid *you*, or have even ostracized you. Whether your illness is physical, mental, or psychological, you can't do the things you used to do, or function as you used to function. So emotionally and socially, your life has also suffered. What I want you to know is that no matter what disease you are facing, no matter what disorder you are up against, I've got good news for you. God is in the healing business. He is a God who can restore.

Greatness and Weakness in Tension

Look again at Naaman. He's the captain of the Syrian army—courageous, valorous, victorious, and all that—but at the same time, he has leprosy. He has greatness because he's the commanding officer, but he also has weakness because he is suffering from a highly contagious disease. He's got ability, he's captain; but he's also got inability, he's diseased. He's got competence, he's a leader of others; but he's also got incompetence because he's got something he can't get rid of. He's got capability, he's gained one victory after another; but he's also got incapability because he's got an illness for which he can't find a cure.

Perhaps you do not understand what I'm trying to say because you may have not had the experience of dealing with greatness and weakness at the same time. Dr. W. J. Shaw, president of the National Baptist Convention, USA, says that it's doable to go through a period of greatness *followed by* a period of weakness, and it's doable to go through a period of weakness followed by a period of greatness. Those situations are not insurmountable; we can handle them. There's a period of greatness when everything goes fine and is in order, and then it's followed by a period of weakness; but we go through the weak time and become strong again. Even though it may not be easy during the weak times, we can still survive them. Shaw says, however, that it is a very different thing when we are dealing with strength and weakness *at the same time.* We've got competence and incompetence operating simultaneously.

There is a strange tension between ability and inability: I'm able to do so much in one area, but I can't do anything in another area—and it's happening at the same time. So, on one hand, I'm captain of the Syrian army; everybody respects and loves me because I've won victories for the people of God. But on the other hand, I've got leprosy. A lot of us experience competence and incompetence at the same time. So how do you deal with that? How do you handle it when you have greatness and weakness at the same time?

Here's what some people do. They become so focused on fixing their weak area that they never function in the area of their greatness. God is saying to them, "I want you to do this…. I want you to start that…. I want you to help them…. I want you to get involved in that…." "No, I can't because I've got leprosy. There's something wrong with me," they quickly reply. "There's a weakness in me, an incapability in me, so I can't get involved, God. As soon as I fix this weakness, though, I'll start functioning in my greatness."

But there are others who do the exact opposite by focusing only on their greatness, acting as if they don't have any weakness. They are strutting around, acting like the captain of the Syrian army, but those around them want to say, "Maybe you forgot, but you've got leprosy!" It is common today to hear people talk about someone being a "functional alcoholic" or "functional drug addict." People in these categories have a chemical dependency, but they still go to work every day and still pay their bills. They still function; however, they don't focus on fixing their *dys*function.

Not only are there functional alcoholics and functional drug addicts in our society, but we've also got functional liars, functional backbiters, functional fornicators, and functional adulterers. We function in the kingdom of God, but many of us are not trying to work on our disorders. Let me tell you—and I can tell you based on both Naaman's experience and my own—when you've got greatness and weakness at the same time, you can't sit on the sidelines saying, "As soon as I fix it...." Nor do you jump in and try to function without working on your weakness. What you have to do is appreciate the greatness you have without ignoring the weakness you have. You have to live out what is right, while at the same time, work on fixing what is wrong.

A Young Girl's Faithfulness

Remember, it was a young slave girl living in Syria who got Naaman started on his journey to wholeness. She was a servant to Captain Naaman's wife, and she said one day to Mrs. Naaman, "I wish the Captain could get to my Pastor Elisha in Samaria, because Elisha can heal this. Pastor can deliver him from this weakness. Pastor knows how to get this cured." You know what's so special about this? Here's a little slave girl who is not so impressed with Naaman's greatness that she can't see that he's got a weakness.

She says, "I know everybody else celebrates him on the job, at work, and in the community. I know he's just gotten an award for the victories he's won. But I live with him at his house. I'm in the home, and I'm able to see that even though there's a lot right with him, there's still something wrong with him. I wish he could get to my pastor." Likewise, we should never get so blinded by the greatness of certain people that we don't see any weakness in them and therefore can't help them in their area of weakness.

Another thing I like about this little girl is that she obviously didn't spend time criticizing Pastor Elisha behind his back. Here's Naaman, who has got a disease that's affecting him physically, psychologically, and emotionally. But this little girl hadn't been heard talking around the house about Elisha: "Oh, that pastor; he's not anything. He's not this and he's not that. And that temple…they oughta…." She didn't do that. She had been boasting on the things of God at her home, so that when somebody got sick, she could point that person to the house of God to get deliverance. Do you want to know why so many of our family members won't listen to us when they get sick, and we're trying to get them to seek help at the church? If we've been criticizing the people of God, the church, and the church leaders, we can't tell our loved one: "I wish you could get to my pastor." You've already destroyed their credibility, so there is no believability.

Another important factor in this story is that this young girl had obviously established a good reputation for herself in this home. She wasn't even talking directly to Naaman when she mentioned that Elisha could help him. Naaman didn't have to pay any attention when his wife said, "Naaman, our little servant girl said...." Why should he listen to a child? To someone who had no power or prestige? To someone who was at the opposite end of the socioeconomic ladder from him? To someone from a different country and culture? Why would he care what *she* said?

It must be that she had earned the respect of Captain and Mrs. Naaman. It must be that she didn't spend a lot of time chattering about nothing; so when she did say something, people listened. It must be that she had proven herself to be honest and of good character—someone who could be believed. It must be that, even though they were of different social backgrounds, different economic backgrounds, different countries, different educational levels, and different ages, Naaman believed that this little girl cared about him, and would not suggest something that would harm him. It's a good thing that Naaman cared more about curing his illness than he did protecting his pride. Truth is truth; and when we are sick, we had better stop trying to pick and choose the one from whom we will get our deliverance. We need to listen to whomever God chooses to send.

Seeing Is Believing

As members of the body of Christ, we need to be as trustworthy as that child. Our reputation needs to be so positive that when we speak, people believe us.

In fact, they should *see* evidence of our faith, even when we haven't said anything. My wife Sharon just got back from Augusta, Georgia, where our son J. Allen is in school. She was there along with the J.C. Squad, my sons' gospel rap group. She told me, "Jeffrey, the next time you go to Augusta, you've got to go to this seafood restaurant there. Their food is really awesome." I asked, "What about that other place we've gone to that we like?" "Oh, I went there, too, but I just wanted to try something different," she replied. "Well, who told you about this seafood restaurant? How did you get wind of it that it was so good?" I pressed her. "Nobody told me about it," Sharon said. "Then what made you think it was good? What caused you to stop in and try it?" "Well, every time we drove by, we would see people walking out with bags of food. Now, this is a sit-down, full-service restaurant, but when we kept passing by there on the weekend, we would see all these people come out with bags of food. That's why we went in to try it. And we discovered that the food was so good, and they gave us so much of it that we ate till we were full, and the next thing we knew we were walking out with bags of food, too!"

While she was speaking to me, I was thinking that this is the way the church of Jesus Christ ought to be—that even if we don't tell anybody anything, they ought to see us walking into the church, coming out full, and taking something home. What Sharon said was that she saw people walking in empty-handed and coming out with something to take to their homes. When you come to the house of God, no matter how empty you are, if you open yourself to the Word of God, taste and see that the Lord is good, and get filled with the Holy Spirit, you will have more than enough to take home with you. What we get at the church impacts those who live with us at home.

Thank God for Prophets

Naaman's next step was to go to his boss, the king of Syria. He said to the king, "You know that I'm sick, but I've heard that there's a prophet in Israel who can heal people. I'd like to go there." The king responded, "Of course, go! But wait a minute. Let me give you a letter of reference. I'll write a letter to the king of Israel, telling him who you are. Based on my recommendation, you're going to get your healing." The king of Syria wrote the letter, sealed it with his official seal, and gave it to Naaman to take with him. So Naaman went to the king of Israel and said, "I've heard there's healing in Israel, and I've come to be healed." The king of Israel opened the letter from the mighty king of Syria, read it, and replied, "Do you think I'm God?! I can't heal you. You're just trying to set me up. Your king sent this letter telling me to heal you. He knows that I can't heal you, so that would only give you a reason to attack us. As a superpower, you're going to come in here and destroy us because I can't heal you."

But Elisha heard about what was happening. He sent word to the king, "No, King, don't be upset. Just send him to me." You see, Naaman wasn't following the right message. The little girl didn't say, "My government can heal you"; the little girl said, "My God can heal you." Don't confuse the government with God. There are some things the government *can* do and *should* do, and we need to hold officials accountable. There are some diseases, however, that the government can't heal. But the God we serve can heal *all* diseases. We often try to legislate so many things. We want to vote on this issue and pass that law. But some things cannot come through legislation; some things have to come through revelation. Had the little girl been there, she would have told Naaman, "I didn't tell you to go to my politician; I told you to go to my pastor." But God made sure that the prophet Elisha knew what was going on. Elisha had confidence in what God could do, so he told the king, "Send him on over here to me." That's the way the church ought to act: "If the government won't feed you, come on over here and we'll feed you." "If the government won't house you, come on over here and we'll find a place for you."

Humility and Obedience

Now, you realize that Naaman was an influential man. He didn't just walk by himself from Syria to Israel. He came riding in with horses and chariots, along with an entourage of men. The text said he took ten changes of clothes with him. He had silver, gold, a few extra mules, his adjutant, a special assistant, and servants. When he pulled up at Pastor Elisha's house, the prophet looked out the window and saw all that stuff. He then sent his assistant out to tell Naaman to go wash in the Jordan River seven times, and he would be healed. So the assistant went out and said (using our terminology), "My pastor sent me on his behalf to tell you that if you want to be healed, just go to the Jordan River, wash yourself seven times, and you will be healed. God bless you. We love you. We'll be praying for you." Then the pastor's assistant went back into the house. But Naaman went off: "Doesn't he know who I am? I'm Captain Naaman. Look at all I've got. Look how far I've come. The very least Elijah could have done was to come out and meet me in person. I know the pastor doesn't talk to everybody, but I *am* Captain Naaman. He's going to send his assistant out to me when I'm sick, rather than coming himself?" The text says he got so angry that he almost turned around and went back home, still sick.

But his assistant said to him, "Naaman, remember, you came here because you are sick. You didn't come here as 'Captain'; you came here as a leper. Now you're trying to change your mentality from that of a leper to a captain. You're going to miss your cure unless you realize you're still sick." When you go into your church on Sunday, remember why you are there. During the week, you may be the "educated doctor," "noted attorney," "sports star," or "successful businessperson." But you don't go to church because of your title; you go there because you're sick. You've got "leprosy." Don't switch from your personal mode to your professional mode and miss your deliverance.

Dr. Shaw says that Naaman almost missed his deliverance because he was trying to dictate his own terms. He was so busy trying to do it his own way that he almost missed it altogether. What he said was, "Pastor should have come out and said something to me. He should have come out and called on the name of God in front of me. At the very least, he should have come out and waved his hand over me." Then he said in disgust, "And he's going to send me to the Jordan to wash! That dirty, muddy water! We've got better rivers back in Syria than this. How dare he send me to dirty waters!" Naaman almost missed his deliverance because rather than doing it according to the principle of God, as shared with him by Elisha's servant, he wanted to dictate the terms of his own deliverance. You can't tell God how to heal you or when to heal you. All you can do is understand that your overcoming is in your obedience. And if you obey, you *can* overcome.

Stop focusing on the preacher, and start listening to the principle so you don't miss out on the power. Whether the pastor gave you the principle inside the house, or outside the house, it's still the same principle. My mentor once told his church: "I'm not going to tell you anything more in private than I've already told you in public. The Word isn't changing when I'm at your sickbed; it's the same Word." Take the principle that comes from the prophet, obey it, and walk in the power of God.

Think about the irony of Naaman's comments. He's complaining that there are better waters in Syria; the waters of the Jordan are too dirty. But *he's* dirty!

He's a dirty person complaining because he has to go to a dirty place. Today, some people say they won't go to church because the people there are too dirty; they aren't clean like they're supposed to be. Those critics didn't say that at the bar; they didn't say that at the strip club; they didn't say that at the crack house. They just took their dirty selves in there, and came out dirtier than when they went in. But at the church, dirty and imperfect as it is, we can still go in dirty and God can clean us up; He can deliver us. Yes, the church has some dirt in it because dirty people come in, wanting to be clean. Not everybody in the church has been cleansed by God, and, from week to week, we all need to be cleansed again from the contamination we've picked up as we've walked through this dirty world. So there is some dirt in the church, I'll grant you that.

But refusing to come in would be like standing outside Noah's ark, saying, "I'm not going in there. There's too much nastiness in there. You've got too many dirty animals in there." Some folk would rather die than to get into the place that God designed for their deliverance. And why do they keep bringing up alternatives to what the prophet is telling them? The prophet said to wash in the Jordan River, but they're bringing up the Abana River and the Pharpar River. Yes, those are clearer waters than those that flow in the Jordan, but the Jordan River has a history of healing and deliverance.

Think of Joshua and the children of Israel. Do you know how they got to the Promised Land? They passed through the Jordan. Think of Elisha's mentor,

Elijah. Do you remember how he got in that whirl-wind and went up to another level? He went up from the Jordan. Elisha took a double portion of Elijah's mantle, struck the Jordan, and passed over through that same river. So if you want to pass over, go up, and go through, you've got to get to the place that's got a history. Just as the Jordan had a history, the church also has a history. A history of civil rights. A history of emancipation. A history of liberation. A history of deliverance. A history of salvation. A history of prayers being answered. A history of folk being delivered. A history of people being healed. These days, we had better be careful about listening to all these alternative religions, because the *church* has got a history. Don't talk to me about another place! I've got to go to the Jordan!

Naaman goes to the preacher, and then he starts criticizing the preacher. But then his assistant says to him, "Naaman, if he had told you to climb a mountain or fight a war—to do something hard—you would have done it. He just said wash and be clean, but you won't do that. He said believe and be saved, but you won't do that. He said repent and be restored, but you won't do that. You won't do the simple things that God tells you." Naaman said, "You're right. I'll go wash in the Jordan. I don't want to. I don't know how it's going to help to wash in a dirty place. But because God said it, I'll do it."

Total Commitment

You may be ready, too, to say, "If that's the church God wants me at, I'll go to the Jordan Church." But remember that when you get to Jordan Church, you're going to see some mud and dirt, and some nasty situations. But don't just stand there and watch the Jordan; get in it and wash in it. It's not enough to come to church to observe. You're not going to be delivered until you participate. You may have been going to church twenty years, watching other folk. But as soon as you switch from observation to participation, here comes your deliverance, your healing, and your restoration. You've been in the church for twenty years and haven't experienced anything, but a stranger may go into the same church this Sunday and come out saved, delivered, and healed. The difference is that they will go into church saying in their hearts, "I didn't come here just to watch you all; I came to get involved."

The message to Naaman was to dip seven times. You may say, "I went to church, but nothing happened." But you only went once, and you didn't get fully immersed. You see, as nasty as leprosy is, you can't just stick your toe in the water and be clean. You're going to have to get completely in the water. In the Bible, the number seven signifies completion. You need to become completely committed to the church, even as Naaman who, after seven dips, was completely committed to the Jordan.

One day, my garage door opener wouldn't work, and we had to call the overhead garage door people to come out. Of course, before they came I had checked it out. I don't know anything about technology; that's my worst area. But I said to myself, "At least let me make sure the thing is plugged in. I don't want to pay somebody $100 just to come and plug in my garage door opener." The outlet is in the ceiling, and I looked up at it and said, "Okay, it's plugged in." So before I went to work, I told Sharon, "Listen, babe, the garage door people are coming out today to work on the overhead door opener." Later in the day, I called home and asked my wife if the repair people had come yet. She answered, "Yes, they came." "Well, did they get it fixed?" "Yes, they got it fixed. It's working, but they said it really wasn't broken." "Yes, it was. I saw it. I kept pressing the button, and it wasn't opening." "But they said the problem was that it wasn't plugged in." "Yes, it was. I checked on it myself. I looked up and saw it for myself; it was up there." "Yes, Jeffrey, but these are his exact words: 'It was *up* there, but it wasn't *in* there.'" You know why I didn't have the power to open the door? Because the plug was *up* there, but it wasn't *in* there.

It isn't enough to go to church and just sit there. You've got to get plugged into Jesus and plugged into the Holy Spirit. I like the way the old preacher tells it. Naaman got into the water, but nothing happened. Now, all of his entourage was there watching as he was trying to get clean in a dirty place. He dipped a second time; nothing happened. A third time— nothing. Now he was feeling stupid. "This doesn't make any sense," he thought. "I've got leprosy and I'm just dipping in dirty water." But the prophet had said, "Just do what God told you." So, not because he could *see* it, but because of what he had been told, Naaman dipped a fourth time; nothing happened. A fifth time, and nothing happened. A sixth time, nothing. But on the seventh time, when he completely obeyed God, he came out clean!

Obedience Brings Blessing

If you obey God and do what He says to do, He will do the rest. You do what you can do, but God will do the rest. You can't heal yourself, but you can get to the place where you can get your healing, a place where you can get plugged in and obey God.

Before he went home to be with the Lord, Dr. Fred Sampson, a great preacher out of Detroit, said he noticed three cleaning institutions on the corner where his church was located. On one corner was a car wash; on another, a cleaners; on the third corner, a hair salon; and on the fourth corner, his church. One day, he noticed a string of dirty cars pulling up to the car wash. They would go in dirty, but they would come out clean. On the other corner, people were carrying loads of dirty clothes into the cleaners. They would go in dirty, but come out clean. On the third corner, he saw women going into the hair salon. Their hair was dirty, messed up, and looking terrible; but when they came out, they came out clean and looking good.

But then Dr. Sampson got frustrated because he would see dirty people go into the church, but come out still dirty. They would go into the church cussing, and come out cussing; go into the church ungodly, and come out ungodly; go in to the church nasty and come out nasty. He was getting really perturbed. "But then," he said, "it dawned on me that when people went into the other cleaning institutions, they did just what they were asked to do. When they went into the car wash and were told to put their car in neutral, they put the car in neutral. At the hair salon, they were told, 'Lie back and put your head in the sink,' and they did. At the cleaners, they were told, 'Give me your clothes and let me wash them,' and they did. But when people come to church, they want to do their own thing. And then they wonder why they aren't clean, why they aren't healed, or why their situation is the same as when they went in."

Let me encourage you. God wants you to be well, to be restored, and to be whole. You can have the very thing God wants for you, but you have to do it His way. You have to obey God—whatever He tells you to do.

You may not see how it can work, but if God says to do it, you need to do what He says. Don't lean on your own understanding. Don't let pride keep you from getting all that God has for you. Don't refuse to listen to someone different from you. Don't become angry when a pastor or church member sees your leprosy and wants to help you find your healing, instead of seeing your professional title and simply offering you a better seat in the congregation. Don't give up after the first dip. You've got to keep on trusting, keep on standing, and keep on believing. God is Jehovah Rapha.

What some people don't understand is that God, who designed our bodies, has already put within us the capacity to heal ourselves. It doesn't always take a "special word from the Lord" to gain our healing; sometimes it simply takes obeying the word He has already given us.

Proverbs 23:20-21, for instance, tells us: "Do not join those who drink too much wine or gorge themselves on meat, for drunkards and gluttons become poor, and drowsiness clothes them in rags." Yet, many of us who would never even consider getting drunk think nothing about gorging ourselves on food. All that food makes us slow, sleepy, and poor because we have lost our energy. Some of us eat continuously throughout the day, from the time we wake up till the time we go to sleep. Our digestive systems are never at rest because it takes them all night to process the food we've taken in during the day. Then we wake up and start all over again. We must learn to eat for energy, not for entertainment.

The story of Daniel offers us some important practical advice on healthy eating. You remember that Daniel 1:8-14 says he was among the most handsome and intelligent young Israelites taken into the court of the Babylonian king to be trained to serve him. Daniel did not feel that he could eat the rich foods the king had sent to these trainees, so he struck a deal with the guard. He asked for a comparison to be made after ten days—comparing the other young men in this group with himself and his three buddies. During this time, Daniel and his friends would eat only fruit and vegetables, but the others could eat anything they liked.

Verse 15 tells us: "At the end of the ten days they looked healthier and better nourished than any of the young men who ate the royal food."

Psalm 23:2 says, "He makes me to lie down in green pastures." Why would God *make* us lie down? Because He knows rest is good for us. We need seven to eight hours of sleep each night in order for our bodies to rejuvenate themselves, and for our immune systems to operate properly. Many of us are not operating at the top of our game simply because we refuse to lie down and rest. If there is any doubt about God's view on this, we need to recall Psalm 127:2: "In vain you rise early and stay up late, toiling for food to eat—for he grants sleep to those he loves."

The second part of Psalm 23:2 says: "He leads me beside quiet waters." God leads us beside water because our bodies need so much water; in fact, over fifty percent of our bodies are comprised of water. Without sufficient water each day, we become dehydrated and our internal organs do not function as they should. Toxic waste from our bodies is not expelled, and we become susceptible to all kinds of illnesses.

When I first began pastoring Eastern Star Church, there was a young lady who asked me to pray for her because she had been diagnosed with diabetes. Of course, I prayed for her, but the next year, I was asked to pray for her again because she had to have her foot amputated. The next year, I was asked to preach at her funeral. What totally amazed me was that her doctor told me that if she had just modified her diet as he had told her to do, she would still have been alive.

But let me share with you an even more personal illustration. All of my life I have tried to be somewhat athletic. I played sports and thought I was taking care of myself. But one day when I went to the doctor, he told me I had high blood pressure and explained that it is known as the silent killer because without warning it can bring on a stroke or heart attack. He gave me some medicine to take, but within two weeks, I realized I couldn't handle the side effects. Frustrated, I went back to the doctor, who told me I would have to continue taking the medicine, unless I was willing to change my diet and get proper exercise. "You mean," I asked, "that if I eat right and exercise, my blood pressure will go down?" When he responded affirmatively, I immediately changed my eating habits and began exercising regularly. Seven years later, I still have no problems with high blood pressure. This came about, not by a supernatural move of God, but by being obedient to what God had already told me about caring for myself.

Psalm 139:13 tells us, "For you created my inmost being; you knit me together in my mother's womb." This same God who made us is the God who can heal us, restore us, and help us to live healthier lives. Someday, as 1 Corinthians 5:2 tells us, we will be "clothed with our heavenly dwelling," with glorious new bodies God will prepare for us. But as long as we are in our earthly "tents," we should live in these bodies to the fullest extent possible. To do this, we must communicate with our Creator, listen to His instructions, and obey whatever He says to do. He *is* Jehovah Rapha.

III

I Want My Mind Back

³For though we live in the world, we do not wage war as the world does. ⁴The weapons we fight with are not the weapons of the world. On the contrary, they have divine power to demolish strongholds. ⁵We demolish arguments and every pretension that sets itself up against the knowledge of God, and we take captive every thought to make it obedient to Christ. ⁶And we will be ready to punish every act of disobedience, once your obedience is complete. ⁷You are looking only on the surface of things. If anyone is confident that he belongs to Christ, he should consider again that we belong to Christ just as much as he.

(2 Corinthians 10:3-7)

Former U.S. Surgeon General Dr. David Satcher reported that one out of every five people has some mental or behavioral disorder for which they really need to get professional help. That means if there are five people in your family, five people on your job, five people in your pew at church, or five people in the room where you are reading this book right now, at least one of you needs to seek professional help! The surgeon general said it, I didn't. But this illustrates the need for the topic of this chapter: "I Want My Mind Back."

When the apostle Paul wrote this second letter to the church at Corinth, he had a little different twist to it, compared to his first letter. First Corinthians focuses on the people of that church, but this second letter concentrates on the pastor, the preacher, the prophet himself. In the first letter, Paul wrote about the congregation and what they were dealing with in terms of divisions, schisms, and carnality.

But this second letter he wrote is not about the congregation; it's about the clergy. He was focusing on himself because he felt that he needed to make a defense for his ministry and apostolic authority. There were those at Corinth who thought that Paul did not have authority as a minister, a preacher, a pastor, and an apostle. So he wrote to them to defend his ministry.

The Mind and Spirit Connection

As he gets to the tenth chapter, he's dealing with one of the things they were saying about him—that when Paul writes these letters, he's hard, bold, and even harsh, but when he shows up and he's face-to-face with them, he's all timid. They said that proves he's not real in terms of his authority. So Paul wrote to them to explain his authority and why he's harsh when he writes, but more compassionate when he is with them in person. He focuses this chapter on mindset, mentality, and psychology because he understands that spirituality and psychology are very closely related. The mind and the spirit are connected. So Paul is writing to the Corinthians to help them understand that "just like you, we pastors live in this world, too. I don't live in glory while you are struggling here in this world. I don't show up from heaven to come to preach to you. We live in the same world as you do."

The world we all live in, as John points out in 1 John 2:16 (KJV), is made up of nothing but the lust of the flesh, the lust of the eyes, and the pride of life. So there are challenges that we face living in the world as Christian believers. And we do *live* in this world. We aren't going to shut ourselves off, throw in the towel, and hold up the white flag of surrender. We aren't going to walk around in depression and dismay. As messed up as this world is, we are still going to *live* in it.

But Paul says the bodies in which we live and walk in this world have weaknesses, frailties, and frustrations. In these bodies, we face the constant challenges of limitations, temptations, and passions. Since we are living in a world that is filled with the lust of the flesh, the lust of the eyes, and the pride of life, we have to constantly be on guard when facing these temptations, so we can overcome our weaknesses. If we are not careful, the world will influence us, and will affect our mindset. So Paul says that he has been working on winning the battle in the mind.

Now many of us may have difficulty dealing with the topic "I Want My Mind Back" because we feel that we have never lost it in the first place. Even as you are reading this, you may be thinking, "I wish my cousin (or someone else you know) were reading this because he's out of his mind." But while this message may be for other people as well, I believe that God is putting this book into the hands of those He wants to read it. So be open to what God may want to say to you. Now here's the issue: how can we regain something that we think we already have?

In order to get our minds back, we have to realize that we've got some issues with our thought processes. There is a way to determine whether your mind, as God intended for it to function, needs to be reclaimed. Let me ask you a few questions:

- Why did you act the way you acted when that person did what he did?
- Why did you respond like that to her?
- Why were you with that person?
- Why did you go there?
- Why did you smoke that?
- Why did you cuss that person out?
- Why did you fight this person?
- Why did you act like that on your job?
- Why did you do that last crazy thing you did?

We've all got some issues in our minds, and it's not until we come to that realization that we can be restored mentally and psychologically to where God wants us to be.

In the fifth chapter of James, the apostle was writing to a group of people about Elijah, the prophet. The Elijah of the Old Testament was so awesome that some people in the New Testament believed John the Baptist was Elijah reincarnated. But James 5:17 says that Elijah was a man of passions, just as we are. So no matter how great he was, he had the same limitations and weaknesses that we all deal with daily. When John the Baptist showed up, some suggested that he was the Christ. John had to explain that he was not the Light, but he came to point to the Light and be a witness about Jesus Christ. He, too, had the same passions, limitations, and temptations as we do. When Peter was preaching in the Book of Acts, the congregation of people began to bow down to Peter because of his authority. Peter said, "Don't bow down to me. Get up. You're going to bow down to the One I'm getting ready to tell you about." Then he said, "I am a man of like passion, just like you."

So in our text, Paul was trying to get the people of Corinth not to judge him on another level, because he lived in the same crazy world they lived in, had the same passions they had, faced the same temptations they faced, and had the same limitations they had. Even Jesus, the Son of God, full of grace and truth, was born God, but He was born into a physical body, into a body of flesh. And in that body, He had limitations, passions, and temptations. The Bible says Jesus was tempted in every area that you and I are tempted in. He never sinned, but He still had to face the temptation. We have to recognize the mental challenges we are up against, if we are going to get our minds back.

The War Within

Now, watch this. Once I realize that I've got psychological issues I need to come to grips with, I also need to understand that I am in the midst of spiritual warfare. Spiritual warfare is taking place in your life and in mine, but it is not always about Satan attacking us. That is indeed a part of spiritual warfare, and we have to look out for the wiles, schemes, and strategies of the devil, but there is no mention of the devil in this text. How can it be spiritual warfare when there is no mention of the devil? Because the battleground is not external: it's internal. It is a war within, a struggle on the inside.

Paul confessed that he had a war in his members, and the battleground was his mind. He wrote to the church at Rome: "That which I love to do, want to do, and know I'm supposed to do, I'm not doing. But the thing I hate and really don't want to do, and know I'm not supposed to do, that's what I find myself doing" (See Romans 7:15). Let's not act all pious and holy about this. We know that Paul isn't the only one struggling. It's a war within me, and it's a war within you. In this war, the mind is the battleground. So we can wake up in the morning and think, "I'm going to change my life. I'm going to be holy today, to be righteous. I'm going to walk in the anointing and power of God. I don't care if others act like a fool;

I'm going to be what God wants me to be today." But by noon, somebody says or does something, and we start acting the very way we said we were not going to act. The mind truly is the battleground.

I recognize there is a war in Iraq, and I know what's happening in Afghanistan. I know about the unrest in the Middle East and that Iran is making threats. North Korea is saying what it might do. I have not forgotten the unrest in Africa—what's happening in the Darfur region of the Sudan, the Central African Republic, Ethiopia, Liberia, Nigeria, the Ivory Coast, and elsewhere. And I know the challenges facing us right here at home. But what we're talking about here is not happening in some external place. The greatest battle going on is the one in your mind and mine. There's a part of me inside that says I'm going to be holy, but then there is something else that builds up in me that is hellish. One aspect of me wants to be righteous, but another acts wretchedly. One aspect of me wants to do what God wants me to do, but then there's something else in me wanting to pull me away from God. This stuff is not outside, but inside. You can pretend it doesn't exist if you want to, but I know there is a war within—it's spiritual warfare.

A Native American tale goes like this: An elder explained that there are two dogs inside of him, a good one and an evil one. "This good dog and this evil dog are fighting each other trying to control my mind and my choices. The good dog is trying to win and take over the evil dog. The evil dog is fighting against the good dog. And," he said, "it's all taking place in my mind." So somebody asked the Native

American elder, "Which dog is winning?" He replied, "The one I feed the most."

It's the same way with me. If I feed the old, sinful nature by embracing the philosophies of this world, listening to degrading music, and letting the lust of the flesh, the lust of the eyes, and the pride of life influence my thinking, then the evil dog is able to overcome the good dog and gain control of me. But if I feed my spirit, which has been made new through Christ, by praying, reading the Bible, fasting, fellowshipping with the saints, and worshiping Him, then I'm feeding the good dog and I'm able to overcome the evil. There's a conflict taking place inside of me and inside of you. You're not going to get your mind back until you stop blaming other folk for what's happening inside of you.

Now, here's the deal. In the midst of warfare, we need weapons to fight the battles. I love the fact that God hasn't left us without weapons. He knows what we're facing and the wrestling match we go through in our daily lives. He knows what is going on in our heads right now. God says, "I love you too much to let you go weaponless." But we need to understand that He is not going to give us weapons like those of the world. We are Christians, we are believers, we are children of God. God does not want us acting like or thinking like the world. In fact, He says we live in the world, but we are not *of* the world. I live in this world, but I cannot think like this world and behave like this world.

When we accept Christ as our personal Savior, we become soldiers in the army of the Lord. That's why we should not be shocked and surprised when we run into opposition. We wrestle not against flesh and blood, but we *do* wrestle. There's a war, and we're in it. Why then should we be shocked that people are taking shots at us? When we were kids, we used to sing, "I'm a solder, in the army...we've got to fight; we've got to hold up the blood-stained banner, we've got to hold it up until we die." Now that we're adults, we understand about that fight we are in. We're engaged now in spiritual warfare, but we don't act like the world acts in this spiritual warfare.

Spiritual Weapons

The weapons of the world are intimidation, separation, and manipulation. The world tries to overcome you by finding ways to intimidate you, by bringing fear into your life. Then, it tries to manipulate you, exploit you, and separate you from your support system so that you think you are the only one going through something, and nobody else cares. That's the trap of the enemy, and that's how the world operates. But when we fight back—and we do fight—our weapons are not like those of the world. God has not left us without weapons, and they are mighty, powerful, even invincible, for the pulling down of strongholds. Listen to what I'm trying to get across to you. Our weapons are not carnal, but spiritual. That's why I know you can get the victory; that's how I know you can win in this spiritual warfare.

What are those weapons? Just look at this arsenal God has provided. He gave you the belt of truth that you put around your waist that holds everything else in place. He gave you the breastplate of righteousness, so when the world is wretched, your heart is protected by the righteousness of God. He gave you the helmet of salvation so the enemy cannot contaminate your mindset. He gave you the shield of faith, but it won't work if you don't stand behind it. You've got to get behind your faith and take a stand on the things of God. He gave you the sword of the Spirit, which is the Word of God, but the sword won't work if you never pick it up. He gave your feet shoes fitted with the readiness of the gospel of peace. We are not peace-breakers, we are peacemakers. Moreover, He gave you the ability to pray in the Spirit on all occasions. After you read Ephesians 6 and get your belt, your helmet, your breastplate, your shield, your sword, and your shoes, you also need to get your prayer life and continually pray in the Spirit.

What's so great about this is, not only are our weapons invincible, but they are invisible as well. Behind all of the weapons and the warfare is an Unseen Reality, an Unseen Presence, an Unseen Power. Just because we don't see God doesn't mean God is not with us. Just because we don't see the Spirit doesn't mean the Spirit is not in us. He's invisible and invincible. I love those aspects of His nature. Our enemies keep wondering how come they can't get us, why they can't bring us down. They think, "All these ditches we've dug for them, all these knives in their backs. All these lies and rumors we've spread, but there they are, still getting the victory." Our enemies don't understand that just because they don't see God doesn't mean God isn't with us. He's invisible and invincible. Because of Him, you can win the battle.

Right Turns Only

Now, some of us don't understand that God is standing with us as we fight, and don't understand that we have to take our orders from Him. We can win this spiritual warfare, but we have to do it God's way. We can't fight by the world's rules, or abandon God's principles and act like the world, and then expect to win the victory.

Pastor Eric Wiggins is pastor of New Horizons Church, Eastern Star Church's newest church plant here in Indianapolis. It is thriving, and we are excited about what God is doing in that ministry. Pastor Wiggins was telling me that one day when his wife Camille went to the store, she was just going to pick up a couple of things and then come right back. But it was taking her longer to get back than it would normally take her, so he was getting a little concerned. When she finally did get back, he looked out the window and saw that she had parked the car crooked in the driveway. When she came in, he asked her, "Baby, are you okay?" She said, "I'm fine." "Then what took you so long, and why are you parked crooked in the driveway?" She responded, "I'm parked crooked in the driveway because that's the only way I could get the car in the driveway." She explained, "When I came out of the store and started to drive, something inside the vehicle broke. When that happened, I couldn't steer correctly. I could only make right turns."

They later learned that it was the tie rod that broke. (The tie rod of your car is what helps with the steering mechanism so that you can turn right and left and go where you want to go.) Camille said, "Something broke in the vehicle, and that's what took me so long to get home. Because I could only make right turns, I had to figure out a way to get home by only making right turns." So, she proved to us that, even though it may take us a little longer, it is possible to get home by only making right turns.

Likewise, it may take a little longer because you've got to make a right turn and go to college before you settle into a career. It may take a little longer because you're making right turns and are not going to put up with some things others may tolerate in relationships. It may take a little longer because you are making right turns and are going to take time to pray and wait on God instead of rushing to get what you want in life. All these things may take a little longer, but you *can* get home making right turns! You *will* reach your true destination by making the right turns. You won't end up lost or in blind alleys.

Perception Makes the Difference

The weapons we are given, as Paul tells us in 2 Corinthians 10, "have divine power to demolish strongholds." Strongholds are fortresses, partitions, walls, or barriers. We have what it takes to pull down all these things. But how are these things erected in the first place, and why? The text says these walls have been erected to keep out the knowledge of God. Now remember, I'm not talking about behavior; I'm talking about mindsets and psychology. What happens in your head is that strongholds go up; these barriers stand between your mind and the knowledge of God. So you're in a setting where a preacher is preaching, or a coworker is sharing spiritual things with you, or a neighbor is talking with you about God, but you can't get it into your mind. That's because in your head, there are strongholds, partitions, fortresses, barriers, and walls standing between your mind and the knowledge of God. Until you can pull these strongholds down, that knowledge cannot get into your mind.

We have to deal with the strongholds of ignorance, conceit, pride, prejudice, and a number of others. But one of the strongholds that especially must be pulled down is the fortress of wrong perception. It doesn't matter what a preacher is preaching, how much the preacher has prepared, how the preacher is presenting the message, or the anointing that is on the preaching; if your perception will not allow the knowledge of God to get into your mind, the preaching will not make a difference in your life. Nor will a book, a CD, a testimony from a friend—not even the Bible itself.

In spiritual warfare, we're not pulling down people; we're pulling down wrong perceptions. We're pulling down this thought process that tells you what is being preached or taught out of God's Word is not for you. As long as this *mis*perception exists, even though somebody says you can be victorious, you can be successful, and you can be prosperous, you'll fold your arms and say, "Well, it could happen for others, but not for me." That's because your misperception is standing in the way of the knowledge of God, and you've got to pull that down. If you don't get your thoughts right, you will never get that victory you are looking for in your life. Victory or defeat is in your thinking.

Dr. Theron Williams says that thoughts are the beginning of everything. If we don't get our thoughts right, we will never walk into all that God has for us. I'm not talking about behavior now; I'm talking about thoughts. Dr. Williams says you can't have the wrong answer. If you *don't* think you can, you can't; if you *think* you can, you can. Either way, you're right. Thoughts are indeed the beginning of everything. Before the house you live in was built and you could move into it, somebody had to think about it first. Or what about the car you drive? Somebody had to first think about it before it could be manufactured. The clothes you're wearing would not even exist if somebody hadn't thought of them. Even the building where Eastern Star Church meets—if God had not first placed that thought in my head, we would not be meeting there today.

Here's what I'm telling you. If you don't think you can get a degree, you can't get one. If you don't think you can prosper, you can't prosper. If you don't think you can have a healthy relationship, you can't have a healthy relationship. If you don't think you can own your own company, you can't own your own company. But I know there are some reading this book who can testify that God has enabled you to pull down strongholds of wrong perceptions so the knowledge of God can get into your thinking. Nineteenth-century British novelist Charles Reade once said, "Sow a thought, reap a word; sow a word, reap an action; sow an action, reap a habit; sow a habit, reap a character; sow a character, reap a destiny." It all starts with a thought. So, my thinking even dictates my destiny. We've got to pull down these partitions of misperceptions.

I've come to understand that these walls we erect seem to let everything else in *except* the knowledge of God. That's why people can memorize secular songs, but they can't learn Psalm 1. And when we start getting everything in our heads except the knowledge of God, it's no wonder we're losing our minds.

I watch the news all the time, trying to keep up with the relevant issues. But in the process, I listen to so much bad news: this person was shot, the war continues there, a child is kidnapped, and all this negative stuff is happening. I sit there and wonder how in the world a person without Jesus and any knowledge of God can make it with all of this negative stuff getting into their heads. Then it dawns on me: they *can't* make it. They begin to sound like Grandmaster Flash: "Don't push me 'cuz I'm close to the edge/ I'm trying not to lose my head." Just like him, we know this world's like a jungle sometimes, but the way we Christians keep from going under is by allowing the knowledge of God to get into our heads.

Wall of Exception

Besides perception, there's another wall. Even though this one isn't in the text, I think is very real and needs to be brought to our attention. It's the wall of exception. Some of us claim to receive the knowledge of God and claim to get it into our heads, but the problem is that we think we are the exception. We hear, "Bring all the tithes into the storehouse that there might be meat in my house," and somebody says, "Amen. But I'm an exception because I'm a single-parent"; or, "…because I'm on a fixed income"; or, "…because I'm going through financial troubles, so God understands." We've built a wall of exception so that we are not really receiving the truth.

We hear, "Don't be unequally yoked together with unbelievers. If you're a Christian, you ought to date Christians; if you're a Christian, you ought to marry a Christian." Somebody says, "Amen." But then that person goes and marries an unbeliever because he or she thinks, "I'm the exception because after we're married, I'm going to win this unbeliever over to Christ." We've built a wall of exception.

God says He's looking for true worshipers who will worship Him in spirit and in truth. And some of us say, "Amen." But we don't show up to worship; we show up to watch others who are worshiping. That's because we're the exception.

The Word of God is the written, absolute truth. Jesus says, "I am the Truth." He is the Living Truth. Truth is absolute: it works in every situation, in

every predicament and for every person. There are
no exceptions.

Wall of Imagination

Another partition we have to pull down is the
wall of imagination. Second Corinthians 10: 4-5
(KJV) says, "(For the weapons of our warfare are not
carnal, but mighty through God to the pulling down of
strongholds); Casting down imaginations, and every
high thing that exalteth itself against the knowledge
of God, and bringing into captivity every thought to
the obedience of Christ." For so many people, the
word of truth and the knowledge of God cannot get
into their heads because they have erected a wall of
imagination. Until the Word of God and the knowledge of God gets into their thinking, they will deal in
fallacy and fantasy. A lot of people run around in this
world operating on fantasy because they never have
received the knowledge of God, which would help
them to distinguish between fantasy and reality.

There is a young person who feels that way
right now, saying that "I'm a man. I don't care
what anybody says; I'm a man." But actually that is
fantasy. If he's living at his daddy's house, driving
his mama's car, and spending his girlfriend's money,
those are boyish characteristics. Until the knowledge
of God gets in, he cannot distinguish between reality
and fantasy.

That's why some people think they're right when
they're really wrong. Some people think they're
up, but they're down. Some people think they're

in, but they're out. Some people think they're holy, but they're hellish. Why? Their imaginations have erected a wall between the knowledge of God and their minds.

This text speaks of casting down imaginations. The word of knowledge is trying to get into your head, and if you don't get it into your head, you're not going to be able to distinguish between reality and fantasy. If you're operating on imagination, there will also be high things in your mind that exalt themselves against the knowledge of God. Imagination not kept in check exacts a high cost, and there are high consequences. Friendships have been lost because somebody imagined something that really wasn't there. Families have been destroyed because one of the partners was imagining something that wasn't even taking place. We have to cast down these vain imaginations.

One of the major reasons people in the Bible got in trouble was because their imaginations went unchecked. Think about it. Lucifer imagined that he would be higher than God. The next thing we know, he's falling from heaven. Saul, jealous of David's victories in battle and his popularity among the people of Israel, imagined that David was plotting to overthrow him. His imaginings led him to try to kill David, and he ended up killing himself after being critically wounded in battle. Judas, one of those allowed to be in Jesus' inner circle, imagined what it would be like to have money. Even though it meant betraying the One who cared most about him, he turned Jesus over to His enemies; but then the reality of what he had done displaced his imagination, and he committed suicide. Imagination, if it goes unchecked, will get you so messed up that great troubles come as a result, which leads me to ask you this: What have you been imagining? What have you been thinking about?

Taking Thoughts Captive

You've got to keep your imaginations in check to let God's truth get into your head. The text says that after you cast down imaginations, you take thoughts captive. Right now, someone is feeling good, thinking, "Okay, finally, I'm casting down these imaginations, pulling down these wrong perceptions, pulling down walls of exception, so now the knowledge of God is getting into my head and everything is fine." No, you've still got some thoughts clamoring for your attention. Paul tells us then what you have to do: you have to take your thoughts captive and make them subject and obedient to Christ Jesus. There are thoughts that get in your head that you just can't allow to run free.

Now, don't try to tell me that all your thoughts are holy and righteous. In my own life, sometimes I'm trying to worship or pray, and then a thought comes out of nowhere. I can't just let that thought have free rein. I have to take that thought and put it in captivity. I've got to incarcerate that thought, because if I let that thing run free, then I'm going to be doing something crazy; I'm going to lose my mind.

So, just as soon as these thoughts come, you've got to take them captive. Don't sit there and enjoy them for a while. You can't say, "I'm not going to do anything with it; I just want to consider it for awhile." No! You've got to *immediately* take the thought and incarcerate it until you can subject it to the obedience of Christ. So, watch this. You confine the thought until you can domesticate it.

You may have a dog that is house trained. As soon as you got the dog, he tried to run free in the house, but you couldn't let him do whatever he wanted because he was going to make a mess and tear things up. So you didn't get rid of the dog, but you kept him in a special pet crate as you trained him to be submissive and obedient. Then you could let him out because he was domesticated. But you weren't able to domesticate him until you first restrained him. Once he was obedient, he could move throughout the house without making a mess. That's the same thing you have to do with your thoughts. You've got to confine them in order to domesticate them so that they will be obedient to Christ.

How We See God and Ourselves

Once the walls are cast down and my thoughts are in captivity, the knowledge of God is able to get into my head; now I know more about God. What I discover is that my theology (what I believe about God) shapes my mentality. What I think about God greatly affects my thought process. Theology shapes my family, my social life, and my economy. When

I can get the right thoughts about God, when I can learn the truth about God, it influences every area of my life. I'm not trying to do right because I'm afraid of what someone else is going to say or do; I'm trying to do right because I understand who *God* is. He's God all by Himself. He's the God who loves me. He's the God who sent His Son for me. He's the God who will lead and guide me.

Our theology shapes our mentality, so once we think rightly about God, then we've got to learn to think rightly about other people. Jesus said, "Don't come to the altar trying to offer your gift to God while remembering that you've got a problem with your brother. Leave your gift at the altar, go find your brother, get that straight and you'll discover the way is more clear." (See Matthew 5:23-24.) Whatever we think about someone is how we'll treat that person. Even though we don't say it, if we *think* someone is inferior to us, we'll *treat* that person like he or she inferior to us. If we think someone is worthless, we'll treat that person as having no value. So, we've got to learn how to esteem other folk higher than ourselves. We've got to learn how to edify and build up others. We've got to learn to treat others the way we want to be treated.

Then we've got to think rightly about ourselves. We've got to get this self-esteem issue straight. We've got to think correctly about God and correctly about ourselves. Someone has suggested that whenever there is an issue in a relationship, insecurity is always a reason. This is true whatever the relationship may be, whether it is husband/wife, boyfriend/

girlfriend, parent/child, worker/coworker, or supervisor/subordinate. Whenever there is an issue, the reason is always insecurity, because I can't get along with you if I can't get along with myself. How am I going to live with you if I can't live with me? You've got to realize, once you have the knowledge of God in your head, that you are fearfully and wonderfully made: that it is He who has made you and not you yourself. You've got to understand who you are.

There is a connection between this and getting your mind back. In verse 7, Paul says, in effect, "You're just looking on the outside. You've got to understand that if you think *you* belong to Christ, *I* belong to Christ, too—just as much as you do." Back in Romans 8:5-6, Paul explains that when we are living by the Spirit of Christ, our minds are healthy and at peace: "Those who live according to the sinful nature have their minds set on what that nature desires; but those who live in accordance with the Spirit have their minds set on what the Spirit desires. The mind of sinful man is death, but the mind controlled by the Spirit is life and peace." Paul would have acknowledged, "I would have lost my mind by now had it not been for the relationship I have with Jesus. Because I have opened my heart to Him, and my mind to the knowledge of Him, my mind is controlled by the Spirit; therefore, it is a mind of life and peace."

It is important for us to recognize who we are in Christ and to know where to find our identity. One day last year, my wife and sons were at an airport getting ready for their return flight to Indianapolis. As they got ready to check in, Sharon suddenly could not find her identification. Realizing she would not be allowed to board the plane without an ID, she searched again and again through her purse and all of her pockets, but it was nowhere to be found. Even though she was at the airport, she was not going to be able to get to her final destination because she had lost her identification. But then our son Jordan remembered something and said, "Check your Bible." She looked and, sure enough, her ID was right there. She had forgotten taking her ID out of her purse and putting it in the Bible she was carrying so that it would be handy when she needed it. My point is that my wife found her identification in the Bible. We, too, need to look for our identification in the Word of God. We need to know who we are as God sees us.

Not Alone in the Fight

Notice, too, the "we" language Paul uses in the 2 Corinthians 10 text. Paul says, "*We* live in this world...*we* fight...*we* demolish strongholds...*we* take our thoughts captive...and *we* belong to Christ." We will be so much stronger in this battle over our minds if we stop trying to battle alone and begin fighting together. Everyone who comes to Christ is immediately part of the family of God and the body of Christ. God knows we can't win wars by ourselves.

I encourage every Christian to have an accountability partner. We each need someone who is filled with the Holy Spirit, holding us accountable. We need someone who can speak directly to us, honestly to us, and openly to us. We need somebody who can say, "Now you know you're not supposed to be acting like this. I know they did that; but you know you're a Christian and you know what God is doing in your life, so you can't take things into your own hands...." We need each other to deal with the spiritual warfare we are facing so that we can overcome. It is about *us* helping each other. When we understand that principle, we also can start to help our kids bring down these barriers in their minds, We can teach them not to allow music, movies, the media, or their peers to erect these barriers in their heads that keep them from understanding the truth of who God is and who they are.

Before fighting Gwendolyn O'Neil in South Africa, boxer Laila Ali was called to the sidelines by her staff and told that the crowd expected her to lose because of who her father is. But then they assured her she was not going to lose the fight for precisely that same reason: "Now, Laila, you are the greatest, and you can't lose *because* of who your father is!" Laila went into the fight and beat O'Neil, knocking her out in just 56 seconds in the first round. In the post-fight interview, in the spirit of her father, who is the greatest fighter of all time, Laila said, "You know, I wanted to give you all at least two rounds, but I just didn't know how great I was."

Let me tell you something. You may have been spending too many rounds in a dysfunctional relationship. You may have spent too many rounds with addictions. You may have spent too many rounds with low self-esteem, thinking negatively about yourself. You need to learn how great you are. You need to know that your greatness lies in who your Father is. God is the greatest of all time, and He's your Father.

The next time you feel as though you can't go on, I want you to know that those who hate you don't want you to make it. In fact, they will try to tell you that you *can't* make it. But you *can* make it because your Father is the greatest of all time. And I'm not talking about Muhammad Ali: I'm talking about God, who is God all by Himself.

God has highly exalted Jesus and has given Him a name that is above all names, that at the name of Jesus every knee shall bow and every tongue shall confess that He is Lord. (See Philippians 2:9-11.) In John 16:33, Jesus said, "I have overcome the world." If you're in Jesus and He has overcome the world, you've already got the victory. You've got to walk like you've got the victory, talk like you've got the victory, and live like you've got the victory.

IV

I Want My Stuff Back

¹David and his men reached Ziklag on the third day. Now the Amalekites had raided the Negev and Ziklag. They had attacked Ziklag and burned it, ² and had taken captive the women and all who were in it, both young and old. They killed none of them, but carried them off as they went on their way.

³When David and his men came to Ziklag, they found it destroyed by fire and their wives and sons and daughters taken captive. ⁴So David and his men wept aloud until they had no strength left to weep. ⁵David's two wives had been captured—Ahinoam of Jezreel and Abigail, the widow of Nabal of Carmel. ⁶David was greatly distressed because the men were talking of stoning him; each one was bitter in spirit because of his sons and daughters. But David found strength in the LORD his God.

⁷Then David said to Abiathar the priest, the son of Ahimelech, "Bring me the ephod." Abiathar brought it to him, ⁸and David inquired of the LORD, "Shall I pursue this raiding party? Will I overtake them?"

"Pursue them," he answered. "You will certainly over-take them and succeed in the rescue."

   [18]David recovered everything the Amalekites had taken, including his two wives. [19]Nothing was missing: young or old, boy or girl, plunder or anything else they had taken. David brought everything back.

(1 Samuel 30:1-8, 18-19)

All of us know what it's like to have had some-thing and then lost it. All of us know what it's like to have had something that was significant—if to no one else but to us. We had it, but now it's gone. It was of value and worth to us, but now we don't have it anymore. All of us know what it's like to have once possessed something we don't possess anymore. We lost it.

For somebody, it was a job. You were doing great on that job. You were moving up the corporate ladder of success, and then that company began to downsize and right-size. You just didn't fit anymore, so they laid you off. For somebody else, it was a relationship. You were not married, but that relationship was very significant. All of a sudden, it ruptured. For somebody else, it was your marriage and family. Everything was running smoothly. You loved them, and they loved you. Everything was going fine, but then there was friction and a fracture occurred in your family. For somebody else, it was an educational opportu-nity. Doors were opening, but then things began to happen. You didn't make the required GPA, or you dropped out for a semester and lost a scholarship. For somebody else, it was money. Money was coming in, so you were investing here and saving there. But then the stock market fell and 9/11 happened. Now the things you used to have, you don't have anymore.

If you know what it's like to once have had something and then not have it anymore, then you know what David is going through in this text. In 1 Samuel 30, David had been *anointed* king, but not yet *appointed* king. God had anointed him in 1 Samuel 16, but has not yet appointed him by 1 Samuel 30. Saul is still the king of Israel. David had been with Saul. He had been at the palace helping Saul, blessing Saul, winning battles for Saul, and calming Saul with great music. David had served Saul, but now Saul is trying to kill David. The very one David tried to help is now trying to hurt him. The very one David tried to bless is trying to curse him. The very one whom David was lifting up is now pulling him down.

So David runs from King Saul, at first trying to hide in Israel. But how can someone as popular as David hide in Israel, especially when the king, who has authority over Israel, has put out an all-points-bulletin (APB) on him? Anywhere David went, there would be somebody willing to turn him in to King Saul. So finally David said, "I've got to get out of Israel."

Hiding with the Enemy

So David left and hid in a place called Ziklag, a town among the Philistine people. The Philistines had been enemies of David from the time he could remember. David, you recall, had even killed Goliath, the champion of the Philistines. But since he was trying to hide from Saul, who had authority over all of Israel, David had to go somewhere that Saul wouldn't find him. He ended up in Ziklag, hiding among the Philistines, his enemies.

Now he has this relationship going with King Achish, one of the leaders of the Philistines. He is letting David and his band of six hundred men hide out in a little town called Ziklag. These men have their wives and children there, and nobody is bothering them. Nobody is stalking David; he's just biding his time. Three years have passed, and everything is fine. He's living in peace. He's had no problems because Saul hasn't been able to get to him.

But then the Philistines wage war against Israel. They call for every man from among the Philistine people to gather together for battle. That would include David and his six hundred men. Now David doesn't want to fight Israel: they are his people, his family, his friends. But he can't tell King Achish and the Philistines, "I don't want to fight against my people," because they would think he is disloyal and might take Israel's side against them. So now he's *acting* like he wants to fight, but he really doesn't want to. He's trying to tell King Achish, "I've got your back. I'm going to battle with you, and you can count on me and my six hundred men."

Watch what happens. The Philistines begin to line up in rows of a hundred men, and a thousand men. At the end of the battalion, here comes David and his six hundred men, lining up with the Philistines, getting ready to fight against Israel. Even though David doesn't want to fight, he keeps telling everybody: "I can't wait to go to battle. Why do you have us in the back?" He is just bluffing because he doesn't want King Achish to know he really doesn't want to fight.

Have you ever acted as though you wanted to fight when you really didn't? Maybe it was a fight on the playground when you were a child. It was a situation you really didn't want to get into, so you were looking for somebody to grab you and get you out of there. You were hoping, "Please, God, let somebody grab me." But then when they grabbed you, in order to save face, you pretended to protest, "Let me go! Let me go!" Come on now, you know what I'm talking about.

Likewise, David wants out of this fight, but he just can't figure out how to make that happen. The leaders of the Philistines have one final meeting before battle, and David's name comes up. King Achish says, "You can count on David. That's my boy. He's not going to let us down." But his advisers reply, "King, I'm sorry, but he can't fight with us. As soon as we get in battle, he's going to turn on us, and this isn't going to be good."

Everything Is Lost

So Achish goes back to David and says, "Look, man, I'm sorry. I tried to get you in, but they aren't going to let you fight with us." Inside, David is shouting and happy. But outside, he is saying, "What?! I've got your back; you can count on me." Then with feigned reluctance, he and his men head on back home to Ziklag, which is eighty miles away—a three-day journey. As they go, they are rejoicing and thanking God that they didn't have to fight. They didn't have to worry about the situation; instead, they could go back and take it easy at Ziklag. But when they get back to Ziklag, David and his six hundred men find out that their wives and their children have been taken captive by the Amalekites. Their houses have been destroyed and all their possessions ripped off. Their loss was so bad that the text says they cried until they had no more power to cry. In other words, they cried until they couldn't cry anymore.

Can you imagine this ending to their three-day journey? They go eighty miles thanking and praising God for what He brought them out of, only to get back home and see their houses burned down; all their belongings stolen; and their wives, sons, and daughters are now in bondage to the Amalekite people.

Let's pause here for a minute because there is a word in this passage for men. Take note that the enemy, the Amalekites, didn't come in and conquer Ziklag until the men left. As long as the men were there, the enemy didn't come in. But as soon as the men were gone, it only took the enemy three days to take away their wives, their sons, their daughters, and all that they owned. In three days, everything they had built up over the last three years had been taken away, but it didn't happen until the men were not present.

That's a word to us, brothers, that when we are out of place, our children are going to be displaced. While David and his men were lining up with the enemy—with people they shouldn't have been with, in a place they should not have been, doing things they should not have been doing—that's when the enemy came in and took all their things. Men need to stay in their place in order to keep their families from being *dis*placed. We need husbands who will be present for their wives. We need fathers who will be present for their children. Because when you're not there, your children are in danger of getting into bondage.

Sociologists and psychologists are telling us about how damaged children can become when their fathers are not present in their lives. That's why so many of our kids are strung out and messed up. That's why they are turning to drugs and alcohol. That's why they're in bondage to poverty and ignorance. They need the nurturing care of their fathers. Even some of us adults have got some issues because our daddies weren't in our lives. We need some men to stop going AWOL (Absent Without Leave) and get back in place.

Choose Your Response

So David and his men return to find out that all their stuff is gone, along with their wives and children. The example of David and his men offer us two alternatives for responding whenever our things start disappearing, our family isn't what it used to be, our marriage is all messed up, our children are in bondage, and our money is gone.

The first option is to respond emotionally. The text says the six hundred men cried until they could not cry anymore. They cried until they didn't have power to cry. But I want you to understand that when they got through crying, their stuff was still gone. Emotion doesn't bring restoration. Now, I'm not telling you not to cry. I don't believe that not crying is a sign of strength. Sometimes you hear people say, "Be strong, don't cry," but that's not a sign of strength. Your crying gives you an emotional release, as well as an opportunity for God to wipe those tears away. Revelation 21:4 talks about a day when God shall wipe away *all* tears from our eyes, but even now, He responds to our tears. Have you ever been in a crying situation when God showed up and began to wipe your tears away? I'm not saying, "Don't cry." I'm saying that can't be your *only* response. Crying and throwing a pity party are not going to correct your situation. That's just an emotional response.

Not only were the men crying, but then they started to blame David: "If it hadn't been for David, we wouldn't be in this situation." Wait a minute, now. They came to David discontented, depressed, and in debt. (See 1 Samuel 22:2.) David is the one who brought them prosperity. Now they're saying he's the one who brought this misfortune upon them. You see, when we start blaming everybody else for the things that we go through, that is an emotional response. At some point, we have to take some of the responsibility. We have to acknowledge that we're in this situation because of choices *we* made. Some people would rather just sit back and complain: "The society's so messed up." "This community isn't this…the politicians aren't that…the president should have done this…if my Daddy had been there…if my mother hadn't been strung out…if my boss hadn't been crazy…." It's always somebody else's fault. That's an emotional response which isn't going to do anything for us.

Watch this. They said, "We're going to stone David." Now, why were they thinking that killing somebody else was going to bring healing to them? Hurting somebody else wasn't going to make them feel better. That was an emotional response.

Instead of responding emotionally like the six hundred men, we need to respond to our trials and troubles spiritually, like David. Look at his situation. His wife and children are gone; Saul, whom he loved and served, has gone crazy; he's a refugee out of Israel; all the people around him are grieving; he's lost his house and all his possessions; Saul's people are trying to kill him; his own people are talking of stoning him; and he can't depend on anybody. Look at what the text says in verse 6: "…but David encouraged himself in the Lord his God," (KJV) or as the NIV puts it: "But David found strength in the Lord his God." This is the spiritual response.

We need to learn to do what David did. When we lose the stuff we used to have—the job's not there, the family's not there, our relationship with our kids is messed up, our boss has to let us go—we need to learn how to encourage ourselves in the Lord. David didn't turn to drugs, alcohol, sexual promiscuity, or other indulgences to deal with his sorrow. Instead, he realized that "no matter whatever else I've *lost*, I've still got what I had with God. He's still my Jehovah. He's still my Elohim. He's still my Jehovah Jireh.

He's still my Jehovah Shalom. He's still my God. You can take my house, you can take my car, you can take my clothes, or you can repossess my things. I can even lose my family, but you cannot take away my relationship with God." So "David found strength in the Lord his God."

Encouraging ourselves in God is something we all need to learn. People should see the difference between the ways saints and sinners respond to bad news. I'm sick of the world thinking that sinners and saints are in the same situation. Sinners can dress like saints, carry a Bible, wear a cross, and go to church, but that doesn't make them saints. Saints and sinners are not the same. Saints need to show the world that their God gives them strength when hard times come.

Remember, in the midst of all of David's troubles, he knew that he had been anointed back in chapter 16 of 1 Samuel. This anointing from the Spirit of God is still with him. So he could think like this: "Even when I go through what I'm going through, I've still got God's Spirit. That's what separates me from sinners. They can put on the same clothes as I do, carry a Bible, wear a cross, and go to church, but they don't have what I've got on the inside. As long as I have God's Holy Spirit, I can encourage myself in the Lord my God."

How to Encourage Yourself

You may say, "Tell me, how can I encourage myself? My family's gone, my job is gone, my money's gone, nobody wants to be with me, and some folk are trying to hurt me." Don't forget, though, if you are a Christian, you've got the Holy Spirit living within you. When you accepted Jesus Christ as your personal Savior, at the very moment you believed, His Spirit took up residence within you. As long as you have the Holy Spirit within you, He will continually sanctify you and set you free. God will speak to you—comforting, helping, and encouraging you.

There is something relatively new in the world of sports. There are now infusion basketballs, infusion footballs, and infusion soccer balls. If you are old school, you may not know what that means, so let me explain. Whenever a basketball loses its bounce because some of the air comes out, or whenever a football begins to go flat because some of the air has seeped out, or whenever a soccer ball loses some of its kick, it becomes worthless, unable to fulfill the purpose for which it was created. So, how do we deal with that loss of air? Back in the day, we used to have to go find an air pump and an air needle. Then, from outside the ball, we would have to pump the ball back up to give it back its bounce. It's not like that anymore with the new infusion balls. They look just like the ones from the old days that we played with, but they really aren't. When the ball starts to go flat (as it will do), we can release the little micropump inside, pump it back up, and then the pump goes back into the ball. Everything it needs is already inside.

I may look just like a sinner, and a sinner looks just like me; but when life begins to take the air out of us, that other person has got to find something outside of himself to help him cope with the losses.

Not me! I turn to that which is inside of me. It's the Holy Spirit who gives me my bounce back!

At some point in our lives, just like David, we're going to have to minister to ourselves and encourage ourselves in the Lord our God. The folk David used to count on were going through the same things he was. Their families were gone, their jobs were gone, their money was gone, and they were in the same situation. Therefore, the people he used to count on, he couldn't count on anymore. The places to which he used to turn had been burnt down. So now what was he going to do? He had to minister to himself.

There is going to come a day in your life when you are not going to be able to depend on your mommy and daddy. I know they've always been there for you. But there's going to come a day when you go through something, and they aren't going to be able to help you. You've always been able to turn to this preacher or that pastor, or this teacher or that mentor, but there's going to come a day when they won't be able to help you. I know you may not believe me right now if everything is smooth and calm and you're just taking it easy. But there's going to come a day that you're going to have to minister to yourself.

Now, I don't know if that meant David stood in front of the mirror, looked at himself, and said, "The Lord is my shepherd, I shall not want…. Yea, though I walk through the valley of the shadow of death, I will fear no evil for You are with me." (See Psalm 23.) I don't know if he stood in front of a mirror and said, "The Lord is my light and my salvation. Whom shall I fear? The Lord is the strength of my life. Of whom shall I be afraid? When my mother and father forsake me, then will the Lord take me up." (See Psalm 27.) I don't know if he stood in the mirror and said, "I will bless the Lord at all times. Everything is gone. All I've got is my praise. I *will* bless the Lord at all times; His praise *shall* continually be in my mouth." (See Psalm 34.) I don't know if he stood in the mirror and said, "All I've got is my breath. Let everything that hath breath praise the Lord." (See Psalm 150.) You are going to have to minister to yourself.

You've been so busy counting on somebody else. Right now, though, it's just you and God. But you and God make a majority, so together you can handle anything in your life. Just you and the Holy Spirit are enough. In 2000, Venus Williams became the first Black woman to win a Wimbledon championship since Althea Gibson in 1957 and 1958. She won her first U.S. Open, along with an Olympic Gold medal in Sydney, Australia, during the same year. After winning her second Wimbledon title in 2001, she was asked a question at a press conference that I'll never forget: "It appeared as though the fans in the stand were for your opponent and against you. It seemed like they wanted your opponent to win more than they wanted you to win. Did that affect your play on the court?" Venus replied, "If you have been following my career, you would notice that when I'm playing, most of the time the fans are for the other person, for my opponent. But it doesn't bother me because I don't need them to want me to win. I want to win bad enough for myself, and if I want it bad enough for me, it doesn't matter who else wants me to have it or doesn't want me to have it. I'm playing to win."

It doesn't matter who's for you or who's against you. If you want it bad enough for yourself, you can still get your stuff back. When Venus made that statement, it was during the time that her father used to hang out in the stands, dancing, laughing, and acting crazy. Do you remember that? So even when all the fans were against her, her father was for her. If you are for you, and your heavenly Father is for you, you can still get your victory.

A Spiritual Response

David responds spiritually by going to see Abiathar, his priest. Look at what he requests from him: "Pastor, I need for you to give me your ephod." Give me your ephod? I thought he was going to go and ask the priest (his pastor) to pray for him. I would have expected him to explain, "Pastor, I need you to pray for me. I'm going through a lot. People are trying to kill me, and my family's been taken captive. I've lost everything. I need for you to pray for me." But David didn't ask his pastor, the priest, to pray for him. That's because the priest was already praying for him. That's the job of the priest—to go to God on behalf of the people. What David was saying in effect was, "I know you're praying for me. I want you to give me your ephod."

An ephod was the vestment for the priests; it was their uniform. After they dressed in all their other attire, one of the last things they would put on was the ephod, a long, vest-like garment. They donned it before entering into God's presence. Then they would go to the Lord in prayer and begin to minister to Him. In essence, David was saying he didn't want Abiathar to stop praying for him, but he also wanted to be able to communicate with God for himself. So, he wanted his pastor to give him the ephod, the thing he used to get to God: "I want you to give me the very thing you have that you use to get into God's presence. Because I don't just want you praying for me; I need more than that. I'm facing some stuff that I need to pray for myself. So give me what you have so that I can do what you do."

Likewise, as a pastor, my job is not to babysit the people in my congregation. It isn't my job at every moment to take care of them, to do this and that for them, to talk to God for them, to fast for them. I do all that (care for them, pray for them, fast for them), but that isn't my only job. My job is to empower them, equip them, and enable them. What about the days they can't get to me? What about the stuff they're never going to tell me? So I have to give to them— and to you, my reader—what I use so that you can do what I do.

You've got to learn to pray for yourself. I know Mother's been praying for you; Daddy's been praying for you; you're in a praying church. But there's going to come a time when you are going to have to pray for yourself. Intercessory prayer is very important, and I don't want to belittle that. I can go to God on behalf of those in my church and, based on *my* faith, *they* get blessed. You can go to God on behalf of a loved one and, based on your faith, that person gets blessed. Again, intercessory prayer is important, but there is nothing like personal prayer, praying without ceasing, and going to God for yourself. When you go to God for yourself, your prayers touch three worlds at the same time. Whenever you pray, your prayers go up to God in worship, out to humanity in work, and down to Satan in warfare. Yet some of us still don't pray for ourselves, and we wonder why nothing's happening.

The moment you begin to take your concerns and requests to the Lord in prayer, God begins to move on your behalf. Watch David. When he started to pray in verse 8, look at what he said to God: "God, should I pursue the Amalekites or not?" God said, "Pursue them." "Will I overtake them?" God said, "You shall overtake them, and you're going to get all your stuff back." David was asking, "God, should I pursue the stuff I lost or not? I had it; I lost it. Should I go after it?" God said, "Go after it." "Now, God, if I go after it, will I get it back?" "You will overtake them, and all that you lost, you will get back."

David didn't go to God and start asking Him for everything on his wish list: "God, I lost my old house; give me a new house. I lost my old wife; give me a new wife. Those kids are crazy; give me new kids." No, this isn't a Christmas list that he handed into God. He didn't tell God, "Now, by a certain date, I expect all of this to come to me." He didn't go to God to try to change His will: "God, I'm praying until I bend Your will to meet mine. And I'm going to pray until finally I can convince You to do things my way." No, and this explains why *our* prayer life is so messed up. A whole lot of us think that is what prayer is: that if we tell God enough times, we're going to get it. Why? Because *we* want it.

Praying God's Will

What kind of God are you serving that lets you boss Him? You say, "But I've read Psalm 37:4. If I delight myself in the Lord, He will give me the desires of my heart. So if I desire it, He's going to give it to me." Now, let me ask you something. What if you desire something that is not in His will? Do you think that because you delighted yourself in the Lord and you desire something, God is going to give you whatever you ask for, even if it's outside of His will? No, what that text is saying is that if I delight myself in the Lord, He will give me the *desires* of my heart. It doesn't mean He's going to provide for me whatever I desire; He's going to give me the desires themselves. Sometimes, I'm desiring some stuff He doesn't want me to have, or I'm desiring to be with somebody He doesn't want me to be with. So, God says, "Jeffrey Johnson, I love you too much to give you what you're asking for; instead, I'm going to change your desires. I'm going to make it so that you desire what I desire for you."

When you start wanting the same thing for yourself that God wants for you, that's real spiritual maturity. Here's David, who is a man after God's own heart. (See Acts 13:22.) He's praying for God's permission: "Should I pursue them?" Some of us are pursuing some stuff that we don't have God's permission to pursue. Some stuff we've lost needs to stay lost. You're at home crying, "I lost my job. Now I'm out of work." But you were only making $4 an hour at that dead-end job, with no opportunity to go any higher. Some stuff that's lost needs to stay lost.

Some man abused you, harassed you, and mistreated you, but now you're trying to get him back? Some woman you shouldn't have been with in the first place left you? Before you start chasing some stuff, ask God, "Should I pursue this or not?" Because sometimes, God is going to say, "Let it go."

But this time, God gave David permission to go after his stuff. Yet David continued praying, "God, if I go after it, am I going to overtake it? Am I going to get it back?" God responded, "When you go after it, you're going to get it *all* back." What we really want from God is what David wanted. We don't just want God's *permission*; we want His *promise*. I don't want to be wasting my time going after something I'm not going to get anyway. So God says to me: "My promise to you, Jeffrey Johnson, is that if you go after what I've given you permission to pursue, you *will* get it back. That is My promise to you."

Some of you have already received God's permission and His promise, but you just aren't pursuing it. He's already promised that He will meet your needs, but you haven't gone out to get a job. He's already promised you a career over a job, but you haven't put in an application anywhere. He already promised you a company over a position, but you haven't gone after your own business. He's already promised that

He's going to take you higher, but you haven't gotten the training. You've got to pursue what He's given you permission to pursue.

Now, don't misunderstand what God meant when He said, "You're going to get it *all* back; I'm giving it *all* back to you." Let me qualify the word "all." When He said "all," it's all that the Amalekites took with them: their wives, sons, daughters, and the possessions that were carried off. They were not going to get their houses back because they had been burned down; they no longer existed. If something doesn't exist, you can't get it back. I'm bringing this up because some people who read this book may want something so much that they may misunderstand their *desire* for God's *promise*. For instance, someone may think "all" includes going back after an ex-spouse to regain a marriage because "God says I can have it all back." Wait a minute, now. Does it exist, or has it been burned down? Your ex-spouse has already been married to someone else for four years, and they've got two kids. That thing's burned down. It doesn't exist for you anymore. Stop going after stuff that doesn't exist anymore.

Let 'Em Go

But in our text, David and his six hundred men were going after what God said he could have. They got to Besor Brook where two hundred of the men said, "David, we just can't go on anymore. We're tired. We've traveled eighty miles in three days, and we're tired. Not just physically, but we're emotionally tired. Our children are gone. Our wives are gone. We're confused about this whole thing. We can't go any farther." But watch David. He doesn't let that detour him. He takes the other four hundred men and presses on to confront the Amalekites. Think about it. He only had six hundred men to begin with and now two hundred of them quit, so the odds are even worse. But David remembered what God told him: "You can have it all." So David says, in essence, to these men: "Now, I'm going after my stuff. I can have it with you, or I can have it without you, but I'm *going* to have it."

Too many of us continue to let folk who won't go with us keep us from having it. Some of us need to tell that person in our life who keeps trying to keep us from walking with God: "I want so much for you to become a Christian and for us to seek God together. I want you to go to God with me. But, baby, if you aren't going, that doesn't mean I'm not going! I can have it with you or without you, but I'm going to have it." Some of you need to tell some man or woman: "I can have a healthy family *with* you or I can have a healthy family *without* you. But either way, I'm *going* to have a healthy family." Two hundred of David's men said they weren't going on with him. Sometimes, folk who start out with you aren't going all the way with you, but you can't let them keep you from getting what God has for you.

One time Sharon and I flew back to Indianapolis from Miami on Southwest Airlines, and we had a connecting flight in Jacksonville, Florida. When we landed in Jacksonville, the flight attendant announced over the sound system: "For those of you who are continuing on to Indianapolis, this is the plane that you will be on. We are asking you not to get out of your seats. We have some people who are getting off here and others coming on, but please remain in your seats. This is the plane that will take you to your final destination." Then she said, "There will also be a crew change. The crew that brought you from Miami to Jacksonville will not be the same one that gets you to your final destination. But if you will just stay in your seats, this is the plane that will get you to your final destination."

While the flight attendant was talking to the passengers, the Holy Spirit was talking to me. He said, "There are some people who joined the church with you, or got saved with you, but they aren't going as far as you're going." So, sometimes, God has to pull you into a situation to let some folk out of your life, bring some new folk into your life, and even change your crew because the one that's been with you isn't going to your destination. Sometimes you have to let some folk go so that you can go on.

The Power of a Testimony

As they traveled on, David's men came across an Egyptian man who was lying sick in the fields. They brought him to David, who fed him and gave him water to drink: the text says David "restored" him. This is significant because the man hadn't eaten or drunk anything for three days. Sick and abandoned, he was tired, weary, and alone. If anybody could identify with that, it was David. He saw that and restored the man to health. Now mind you, David was on his way to his own restoration, but he still found time to restore somebody else. He may have been thinking, "I don't have everything I'm going to have, but I do have something. I'm going to take the little bit I have and restore *you* on the way to my own restoration."

Now some of us are waiting until we become big and live large before we start doing something in the kingdom. While you're on your way to regaining your stuff, you've got to learn to bless somebody else. As bad off as you are, somebody is worse off than you. As broke as you are, somebody has less than you. As jacked up as your living arrangements are, somebody's are more jacked up than yours. So while you're on your way to getting your stuff back, you need to bless somebody else. If you restore someone else, you're going to reap what you sow, and God is going to restore you.

They asked this man who he was. He said, "I am an Egyptian. I used to be with the Amalekites. I served the ones who destroyed Ziklag, but I'm not with them anymore. I used to be enslaved by the same enemy who has enslaved your children, but I'm not a slave to them anymore."

I love God so much. Just as He did with David, while we're on our way to *our* restoration, God will show us someone else who has been affected by the same circumstances that have affected us. When we hear that someone else has been set free, it lets us know that we can be set free, too. That's why we've got to start telling *real* testimonies. We need some real testimonies from people like this Egyptian, who will say, "I once was under the influence of the wrong people, but I'm not under their influence anymore. I once was in bondage, but I'm not in bondage anymore." We need people who are willing to say, "I was strung out, but I'm not strung out anymore. If God set *me* free, He can set your children free."

Worth Fighting For

When David and his men reached the Amalekites, their enemies were eating, dancing, and drinking—with *their* stuff. They went in with four hundred men to face their enemy. There were more Amalekites than the men David had with him. They were stronger and had more resources. The people with David faced overwhelming odds, but they fought anyhow. The text says when David's men fought, they got their wives back, their children back, and their stuff back. They were teaching us that some stuff you're not going to get back without a fight. You can stay in Ziklag, crying and throwing a pity party, but you don't get any stuff back like that. If you want your family back, you've got to fight to get it back. The enemy took your stuff, so you've got to tell him, "You can't have my stuff. Satan, I want my stuff back." Your family is worth fighting for!

A few years ago in Pensacola, Florida, an eight-year-old boy was out in the ocean swimming when a shark grabbed his arm. The boy cried out, "He's got me!" Without thinking, his uncle jumped into the water and swam out to him. After subduing the six-and-a-half-foot shark, he took his nephew's arm out of the shark's mouth and carried him back to the shore. Here was an uncle who, when he saw that something had got a hold of his nephew, left his comfort zone, and fought something bigger than he was, in an element he didn't know anything about. He wrestled his nephew's arm out of the shark's mouth and swam him back to the shore because he knew *his family was worth fighting for*. Don't walk out of that marriage without a fight! Don't leave those kids without a fight! Family is worth fighting for!

Then David said, "It was God's grace that gave me my stuff back." If you want your stuff back, it's going to happen because of the grace of God. It doesn't matter that your resources are depleted. God's grace is sufficient. It doesn't matter that the enemy is so powerful. God's grace is sufficient. It doesn't matter that you're emotionally weary, you've traveled a long distance, and are tired and in distress. God's grace is sufficient. Trust God to help you get your stuff back.

V

I Want My Family Back

⁸Then the king of Sodom, the king of Gomorrah, the king of Admah, the king of Zeboiim and the king of Bela (that is, Zoar) marched out and drew up their battle lines in the Valley of Siddim ⁹against Kedorlaomer king of Elam, Tidal king of Goiim, Amraphel king of Shinar and Arioch king of Ellasar—four kings against five. ¹⁰Now the Valley of Siddim was full of tar pits, and when the kings of Sodom and Gomorrah fled, some of the men fell into them and the rest fled to the hills. ¹¹The four kings seized all the goods of Sodom and Gomorrah and all their food; then they went away. ¹²They also carried off Abram's nephew Lot and his possessions, since he was living in Sodom.

¹³One who had escaped came and reported this to Abram the Hebrew. Now Abram was living near the great trees of Mamre the Amorite, a brother of Eshcol and Aner, all of whom were allied with Abram. ¹⁴When Abram heard that his relative had been taken captive, he called out the 318 trained men born in his household and went in pursuit as far as Dan. ¹⁵During the night Abram divided his men to attack them and he

routed them, pursuing them as far as Hobah, north of Damascus. [16]He recovered all the goods and brought back his relative Lot and his possessions, together with the women and the other people.

(Genesis 14:8-16)

Nnone of us can honestly put a sign out in our front yard that says, "No hurt here." None of us can place a plaque in our home that truthfully reads, "No pain here." Every family has some hurt somewhere; every home has pain somewhere. There is some type of friction or bondage within every family. And there is no pain like family pain; there is no hurt like family hurt. We run into hurt in a lot of places, but not as much as we can experience in our homes. If you have not experienced pain in your family yet, just keep on living: keep getting up in the morning, keep going through your daily routine, and pain will come into your home.

We are living in a time with so much addiction to so many things that all of us are going to be touched—if we have not been already—by some type of bondage. But I believe that just as Abram went and brought his nephew Lot back out of bondage, God has also given us some liberating principles, along with the power, to restore our families so that they will reflect the relationship that we have with God through His Son Jesus Christ.

Family Pain

I wonder what brings this kind of friction and fracture in families. When we see the birth of our babies, we call them bouncing baby boys or bouncing baby girls. We tell everybody about the joy that we have. But far too often, that joy can turn to pain. When people get married, they have no intention of getting a divorce because they think that they are going to be the exception to the rule. Even though nearly everybody else's marriage is experiencing problems, and so many other marriages have fallen apart, they believe it won't happen to them because they *love* each other too much. Yet their marriage, too, as one of my friends says, "goes from being like *Little House on the Prairie* to *Nightmare on Elm Street*."

So what causes this kind of friction? What causes this kind of hurt, this kind of pain, and the fracturing we see in so many relationships in the family—whether it is husband and wife, parent and child, or brother and sister? What in the world does that? When Genesis 13 opens, Abram and his nephew Lot seem to be doing so well. It's almost like Uncle Abram is the mentor for his young nephew, and Lot seems to be learning much from him. He is benefiting from his uncle. They have gotten away from a place that doesn't believe in Jehovah, so now everything is going well. They have both become very wealthy with their silver, gold, flocks, and herds of animals. In short, they are doing very, very well.

Abram has a relationship with God that is literally second to none. Not only has he moved to an area called Bethel, which means "house of God," but he has built an altar for God. He has gone from having nothing to having everything, including a good relationship with his wife and nephew, so everything seems to be going well. Yet, he still goes to the house of God and establishes an altar, which is a reflection of prayer, sacrifice, and giving to God. At the altar, he calls upon the name of the Lord. I'm impressed with that because a lot of us only go to church when we're hurting. We only call on the Lord when we *want* something from Him. But here's a man for whom everything is going well, and he is still at the house of God—still giving, still praying, and still calling upon the name of the Lord. Yet, even though he is in a right relationship with God, problems still occur within his family relationships. Likewise, just because we have it right with God doesn't mean that we are going to be immune to suffering. Everybody is going to experience suffering.

Separation

So, what caused the problem between Abram and his nephew Lot? One of their problems was money. The number one reason for divorce in America is not infidelity, sexual incompatibility, nor abuse: it involves finances. You may be thinking, "But how could finances bring friction in this family when Abram and his nephew are both rich? What is the problem?" The reason for divorce is not always the lack of money, but what we do with the money we have. The issue isn't that we don't have anything. The issue is that we can't agree on what to do with what we have. That's what happened in this case: there is friction in this family because of finances.

They cannot agree on how to handle the resources with which God has blessed them.

The dispute between Abram and his nephew affected others around them as well; their employees began to fight with each other. But Abram made a decision and said to Lot, "Listen, we're both blessed. There's no need for us to fight each other like this. Here's what we're going to do. You go your way and I'll go my way." (I confess when I was reading this, it reminded me of the script in one of those old westerns: "This town is not big enough for the both of us.") Abram and Lot had both gotten so big that they thought they couldn't live in the same place. In the same way, egos can come between us and our families, if we're not careful. My friend Maurice Watson, pastor of Beulahland Bible Church in Macon, Georgia, says that ego is spelled E-G-O, "**E**asing **G**od **O**ut." Whenever you get a haughty spirit, something bad is going to happen. Whenever you build up your pride, something bad is going to happen.

So here were Abram and his nephew Lot both doing well, but this town wasn't big enough for the both of them. So Abram said to Lot: "You just choose whichever way you're going, and I'll go the other way." Lot agreed, "We're going to go our own separate ways." Division comes when family members decide they can't go in the same direction. Each person wants to have his or her own way. So they say to each other: "If you choose to go left, I'm going to go right. If you choose to go in, I'm going to stay out. If you choose to stay, I'm leaving." Whatever the direction, they aren't going to go together because they each want their own way.

This is what happens in many of our families. We can't stay together because each one of us wants our own way. We keep thinking the other person ought to see it our way and go our way, but the other person is thinking the same thing: "You ought to see it my way and go my way." And whose side is God on?

In the past, when I did marriage and family counseling for church members, I'd frequently have a husband and wife sitting in front of me. After they had fallen out with each other, they were sitting in my office wanting to know whose side *God* was on. Of course, I'd have to help them understand that God wasn't on either side because He has His own side. God doesn't go his way or her way; God goes His own way. So if a couple really wants to get their relationship straightened out, they both need to stop going their own way, seek to know God's way, and follow it.

One day, an old couple was driving down the street. The old man was driving and his wife was sitting over by the door on the passenger's side. They saw a young couple driving in front of them. The young woman was nestled in her man's arms, and they were closely snuggled together. The old lady looked at her husband and said, "I remember when we used to be like that. You used to hug me close, and we rode down the street all cuddled together like that. But now look at us." The old man responded wryly, "Well, I'm still in the same place." Sometimes, we have strayed from God, and we sit there wondering why things aren't the way they used to be. But God didn't go anywhere; He's still in the same place.

Let's say you and a family member have distanced yourselves from each other, but Jesus is in the middle. You *were* together, both of you walking with Jesus and, consequently, with each other. But you've begun to separate from each other, determined to go your own way. Why don't you stop for a minute and figure out God's way? If both of you head in the direction of Jesus, you can't help but come together. If you start getting a little closer to Jesus and the other person starts getting a little closer to Jesus, soon you're going to be heading in the same direction.

Lot's Mirage

But Abram and Lot didn't do it that way. Lot looked up in the direction of Sodom. He didn't go there to check out the culture. He didn't go to Sodom to see if there were any good houses of God there. He didn't go to check on the school systems, the systems of government, or the property and income taxes. All he saw were trees, water, and a garden that looked to him like the garden of God. He was focused on finding a place where he could continue to preserve and accumulate wealth. He was looking for a place that would make him richer. In contrast, look at Abram. The text says that Abram went to Bethel, the house of God, and there he built an altar unto God to pray and to give. He called upon the name of the Lord.

Lot saw the resources for continued material growth. Even though it also reminded him of Egypt, the place from which God had brought him out, all Lot saw was "green," and he wanted it. Abram saw a house of God—a place to pray and an altar upon which to give unto the Lord. Lot moved in the direction of "green" and ended up in bondage. But Abram chose God over "green," and God showed up. Not only did God show up, but He began talking about the blessings Abram was going to receive. He said, "Abram, look all around you; all the land that you see will be yours. When you look at the particles of dust on the earth, that's the number of descendants with which I will bless you." To Abram, who chose God, came blessing. To Lot, who chose "green," came burdens.

Green, as you know, is the color of our currency. Many of us have ignored God and chosen green, yet we're wondering why we're in bondage. Not only is Lot in bondage, but his wife is also in bondage with him. In chapter 13, we see that Lot chose the land that was pleasing to his eyes, a place where he apparently thought he could prosper. He pitched his tent toward Sodom, even though verse 13 tells us that "the men of Sodom were wicked and sinners before the Lord exceedingly" (KJV). Lot chose prosperity over God. He went to live in Sodom even though this was a sinful place—a place that was not conducive to healthy family life, a place that would draw him away from God.

Chapter 14 tells us that an alliance of four kings attacked another coalition made up of five kings, which included the king of Sodom. When those four kings defeated the king of Sodom and his crew, he took off running, leaving the people who lived in Sodom to fend for themselves. The inhabitants ended up in bondage, and their possessions—flocks, herds, silver, gold, everything—were all taken from them. Lot had chosen a place where he could not even defend his family. In such a place, a culture without God, he ended up in bondage, and his wife did, too. He had chosen money over his family. He didn't care that the culture of Sodom was against the family, and that it was a place corrupted by sexual promiscuity. He didn't care that he was living in a place where people chose sexual promiscuity over God's ideal plan for families.

Bondage

Lot's situation is especially interesting when we realize that he didn't end up in bondage because of who *he* was, but rather because of whom he was living among. The foreign kings weren't coming for Lot; instead, they were coming for the king of Sodom and the residents of that city. Lot wasn't from Sodom, but he had chosen to live among Sodomites. He was hanging out with the wrong people; so when they were captured, he was captured. My grandma says that if you lie down with dogs, you're going to get up with fleas. And, my mama says that association brings about assimilation. You've got to be careful who you hang with. The Bible says we are not to be unequally yoked with unbelievers. That means if you're a Christian, you've got to run with Christians. If you yoke yourself with folk who are wicked and sinning—those people who are against God and not thinking about the welfare of their families—the next thing you know is that you'll end up in bondage somewhere. Dogs run with dogs, cats run with cats, horses run with horses, buffalo run with buffalo, fish swim in schools, birds of a feather flock together, and a child of God needs to run with another child of God. If not, you'll end up being treated like the ones you're running with.

Now, you may be thinking this talk about bondage isn't for you because you're a child of God. You regularly go to the house of God. You continually go to the altar of God. You call on the name of God. Your soul is saved. But just because your soul is free doesn't mean you are holistically emancipated. Even though your soul is set free, there may be a part of you that is still in bondage to something. Your soul can be saved, but your mind can still be in bondage. Your soul can be saved, but your lifestyle can be in bondage. Your soul can be saved, but your money may still be in bondage.

Bondage comes in so many forms. If I'm smoking two or three packs a day, I know it's affecting my health and can even take my life. But as long as I keep doing it anyway, I'm in bondage. If I'm doing drugs, I know it is killing my brain cells and having a negative effect on my life. But as long as I'm doing it anyway, I'm in bondage. If I'm getting drunk every day, I know it's affecting my family, my job, my money, and my future. But as long as I'm doing it anyway, I'm in bondage. So these aren't your hang-ups? Well, if I'm caught in gluttony, I'm eating so much food that I know it is hurting my body. As long as I keep eating too much anyway, I'm in bondage. If I'm codependent with someone and I let that person treat me badly, I'm miserable and depressed. As long as I keep allowing it to happen, I'm in bondage.

But bondage doesn't *look* like bondage at the beginning; that's how we become entrapped. You used to play video games and computer games just for the fun of it, but now you find yourself sitting in front of a computer hour after hour instead of spending time with friends and family. You used to occasionally watch television for a little while because it was a way to relax after a hard day at work, but now you spend night after night in front of the TV and have no time to read, no time for church activities, and no time for God. You used to think it was harmless to glance once in a while at magazines on the newsstand that had sexually explicit pictures, but now you have pornographic magazines hidden under your mattress and you're frequenting web sites that feed your obsessive lust. You began as a child telling little lies to keep yourself from being embarrassed or getting in trouble; but now you no longer even monitor yourself, and lies flow from your mouth as easily as the truth. You used to work long hours because you wanted to establish yourself as a good employee, a team player, and one deserving of appropriate rewards; but now, even though your children never see you and you and your spouse no longer even know each other, you continue to work those hours. These are all types of bondage.

You can tell it's bondage if you're on your way to doing it and try to talk yourself out of it, but can't. You're holding a conversation with yourself, trying to stop yourself from doing what you know you ought not to do. But you won't listen to yourself; you do it anyway. So the next day, you wake up asking yourself again, "Why did I do that?" Whatever the source of our bondage, we need to be liberated, emancipated, set free.

Sometimes it isn't us who are in bondage, but someone we love or care for. Abram was not in bondage. He had gotten it right by going to the house of God. He was at the altar of the Lord praying, giving, and calling on the name of the Lord. Evidently, Lot must have gone "left" because it appears that Abram went "right." When Abram went right, God blessed him. But his nephew was in bondage.

Freed to Free Others

The text in Genesis says that when Lot ended up in bondage with the rest of the residents in Sodom, one person escaped, ran to Abram, and said, "I know where your nephew is. I know what's holding him and his wife in bondage." The very fact that one escaped indicated there was a possibility, no matter what, that another could escape as well. In fact, there is no temptation that has seized us except what is common to everybody else, but God is able even with the test we are going through to give us the way of escape. (See 1 Corinthians 10:13.)

Being a witness is so important. The very fact that one person got out is an indication that some-body else can get out. When we start telling people what we've been delivered from, it becomes an encouragement to them. When we start telling the truth about what God has pulled us out of (the things that have held us captive), we offer hope to others who are in bondage. We need to let others know that since God set us free, we're not what we used to be. This will cause others to respond, "Well, if God could pull *you* out, he can pull my son out, my brother out, or my husband out, and my family can be restored." Why? Because one escaped.

Let me assure you of something. Even though Lot, as well as other men, were in bondage, the text lets us know that not every man was in bondage. This one man who had just escaped from bondage went to Abram, who had *never* been in bondage. Moreover, Abram had 318 men with him who had never been in bondage. Sometimes, because our society today is so messed up, there is a tendency for us to overgener-alize that "every man is messed up." No, every man is not messed up. Some people have walked with God since childhood, and He has prevented certain bondages from coming into their situation. Others were in bondage, but they have escaped. Every man is not in bondage.

I love the fact that when this one man escaped, he didn't just go out and do his own thing. He went and told someone who could help get the rest of the captives out. When he got free, he didn't just think about himself. He thought, "Even though I got out, there are still some others locked up, still some others in bondage, still some others whose lives are messed up." We've got to stop our intentional amnesia. Some of us have amnesia and haven't even bumped our heads. We've forgotten where we came from. Some of us, when we get restored and back on our feet, forget there are some folk who are still in bondage. We've got to do whatever is necessary to bring them out. When we come out, we've got to help somebody else come out. You may say, "I would like to help, but I don't know how. I just barely got out myself." Maybe that's true, but you can find somebody like Abram and tell him or her: "We need to do something. I don't have the resources to get them out, but you do." Here's what I'm trying to tell you: even if you can't get them out by yourself, you can talk to somebody who can get them out.

John 8:36 says, "So if the Son sets you free, you will be free indeed." You *do* know that the Son can get them out? So even if you can't do it, you ought to talk to Jesus, because He *can* do it. He can set folk free. And not only that, but He's using a human representative here to whom He has given resources so that He would be able to set somebody free. The man who escaped ran to Abram. He doesn't run to the king of Sodom, because when the attacks took place, the king ran and hid. Even though he knew where Lot and the others were, the king didn't go to get them out. He was there when Lot got in trouble; but when Lot lost everything, the king disappeared.

In the next chapter, the king of Sodom shows up again when Lot is back on his feet.

Follow what I'm saying. When Lot got in trouble, the king of Sodom disappeared. While he was in bondage, you couldn't find the king. But when Lot recovered everything and got back on his feet, the king of Sodom shows up again. Lot was a multi-millionaire. He owned so much stuff that he and his uncle had not even been able to live in the same town. When he had all of that, the king of Sodom knew who he was, but when he lost everything, the king disappeared. Then, when Lot got it back, the king reappeared.

A lot of times you don't know who your friends are until you go through something. Some folk only get with us because of what they think we have; but if we lose it and they disappear, we know they weren't our friends in the first place. Don't show up when your friend has got something and disappear when he loses it, and then when he's got something again reappear like you're some magician. We need to help each other get through whatever we're facing during the rough times.

A Family Response

Abram hears about what's happened with his nephew. I love this because even though this young man Lot was in trouble, it still says he was his nephew. We've got to stop disowning family members when they go through trouble. Abram could have said, "I don't have to help him. I tried to tell him before not to leave. I mentored him. Had he listened to me, had he not made the choice to hang with these folk, he would never have been in this predicament." You see, some of us act like we don't have to help folk because of the decisions that they have made. If I could make all the right decisions, I wouldn't need you. I need somebody who, when I've messed up, can come alongside and help me recover.

Someone may be saying, "Well, if she had not had sex when she was fifteen, she wouldn't be in this situation," like that makes you immune from helping somebody. "Had he not dropped out of high school, he wouldn't have been in this situation." "Had he not stolen...." I understand that those were bad choices, but when people mess up, isn't the gospel message about the restorative power of God—how He forgives people of their sin?

So then, how does it happen? How do we get our relatives out of bondage? The text says we've got to get organized because there's a process to deliverance. Abram had to get organized. He was living near three brothers, so he pulled them together. He had 318 men who were born in his house; he brought them in, too. And these men had been trained. You see, without organization, there can be no emancipation. You may say, "I'm against organized religion." Well, what are you *for—dis*organized religion? If it had not been for organized Christianity, there would have been no freeing of the slaves. Had Black Christians and White Christians not worked together within the civil rights movement, Blacks would still be relegated to going to back doors. Had Blacks and Whites around the world not worked together against the racist system of apartheid in South Africa, Blacks there would still be living in subservience. Abram and his men got organized. I love this because it says Abram went to get the brothers and the firstborn in his household. Now you've got to understand, Abram is the *father of the faithful,* so those born in his household were born into the household of the faithful. We've got to start connecting with Christians, those people who have been born again. He connects with those who have been born of faith: 318 men. They are going to get Lot and his wife out of bondage.

Look at how many men it takes—318. They all pull together to go rescue two people. Now, everybody's going to get set free because of what they do, but they are really going down just to free Lot and his wife. It took 318 people. Do you know why I'm bringing that up? Because there are people who keep telling me, "Your church, with its ten thousand members, is too big." Not if we're trying to rescue people! Maybe they don't know how many families are in bondage. Maybe they don't know how many children are strung out. Maybe they don't know how many cousins are messed up. If it's going to take three hundred of us just to get a couple of people out of this stuff they are facing, think how many it will take to rescue a community—to offer freedom to a whole city of folk. Really, we're not too big; we're not big enough.

Trained for Battle

Not only do we rescuers need to be born again, but we need to be trained as well, just like Abram's men. Some of us think it was enough for us just to come down the aisle and give our lives to Christ. No, we need to be trained because we cannot get people out of bondage if we are not trained ourselves. That's why we need to unite with a church and get involved in its program for new members. Why? Because we need to be trained. We need to participate in Sunday School. Why? Because we need to be trained. We need to participate in Bible studies and prayer meetings. Why? Because we need to be trained. We need to participate in revival services, conferences, and seminars. Why? Because we need to be trained. Don't think you can wait until somebody's in bondage before you get your training. You'd better get trained now so that when your loved ones are taken into bondage, you have the wherewithal to go get them out.

What were Abram's men trained in? The text doesn't say, but it appears that they were at least trained in setting people free. I don't know what kind of training they went through, but they had enough to emancipate somebody other than themselves. The very least you ought to get from church is to learn how to lead somebody else to Jesus Christ. You ought to at least have the basic training to be able to walk up to somebody and say, "If you're lost, I know somebody named Jesus who can save you. All you've got to do is admit that you're a sinner and that sin has separated you from God. But, you know, God still loves you and by calling upon the name of the Lord, you will be saved." That's just basic training.

Fighting in the Dark

Do you know why Abram's men had to be trained? Because when they went to get Lot out, the Bible says they had to fight at night. Let me tell you something. You're not getting your family back without a fight. The enemy is not going to let your family go without a fight. You can sit in the household of faith and pray (and prayer is important); but when you get through praying, you're going to have to get up and fight. Remember that family is worth fighting for.

You cannot just let the enemy step into your situation, tear up your marriage, tear up what you have with your children, tear up what you have with your extended family, and just sit there. You're going to have to fight, and you're going to have to fight on enemy territory. You've got to learn how to fight in the night, in an area to which you are not accustomed. The 318 men born into the household of faith were trained, but the fighting they did was not in the house. The fighting they did was outside the house. It's cool that we go to church to sing, pray, and listen to the Word, but after we get trained in the house, the fighting happens outside those walls. I know we're comfortable in our churches because the lights are on and there are other Christian lights all around us, but the text says they had to learn how to fight at night. We've got to get to the point that we can walk in a dirty world, in a dark world, and tell our family and our friends how important it is to have a relationship with Jesus.

The text says that the men divided when they got to the place of battle. Abram ordered half of them to go one way, and the other half to go the other way. That's one demonstration of the fact that they had been trained: at least half of them were not with Abram, but they still knew how to fight. They didn't say, "Nobody can help me but Abram. If Pastor Abram isn't here, I'm not talking to anybody. Pastor Abram's the one who's got to lead me in this." When you are born again into the household of faith and you've got your own training, you know you can still get the victory even if you don't see the leader.

Watch this. When they go to fight, the text says they fight in the night. I called a former associate pastor today to talk with him about this. Pastor David Page, now senior pastor of New Baptist Church in Indianapolis, served in the military for a number of years. I called him and said, "Pastor, you've been in the military. I know when you are on foreign soil, all of the fighting is not in the daytime. How do you fight in the night when you are in an environment in which you are not accustomed? How do you get the victory on enemy territory—at the dope house, the crack house, or the whorehouse? How do you get the victory when you are in unfamiliar territory, and it is at night?"

Pastor Page told me it is all about the equipment that you are issued when you get into the service. They give you the equipment and then send you through basic training, so that when you get into an environment you're not accustomed to, your brain kicks in and you know how to use the equipment you've been given. I said, "Pastor, I still don't know how you can fight in the night, even if you have the equipment." He said, "One piece of equipment they give you is night-vision goggles. You've got to be able to see in the night if you're going to get the victory."

So what God does when you get saved is that, through His Holy Spirit, He gives you night-vision goggles so that even when other folk can't see, you've got the vision to know what to do. Page continued that not only do they give you night-vision goggles so you can see in dark situations, but they also give you a radio so you can stay in communication with the one giving the directions. He told me that with the radio, you are tuned in on a certain frequency so the enemy cannot hear what you're talking about.

But then Page said something that really blessed me. He said that the radio often changed frequency, so at noon when it's the brightest, you might be on one frequency, but everybody in the same army knows when to change to a different frequency and which frequency to go to. The Spirit was speaking to me as he was talking. Just think. We can call on God in the middle of the night and ask Him to give us direction about the way to handle our situation. While we're at work, we're on one frequency, but when we get home and a family member is acting the fool, we've got to know what frequency to get on. And only the Commanding Officer has the authority to change the frequency. That's how I know it's always out of order for me to cuss someone out, because God is never going to put me on that frequency.

Page said something else that was so meaningful. He said that even if you're wearing your night-vision goggles, and even if you've got your radio and know what frequency to get on, it is still possible to get lost at times because the terrain is so rugged and the territory so unfamiliar. But even if you get lost, everything is still going to be all right because the army always gives you a compass, and you can use it to give you direction. Again, the Holy Spirit spoke to me, letting me know that it is possible for us to get lost trying to find somebody else because we are in the dark and not familiar with the territory. Meanwhile, the enemy is fighting the whole time we're out there. But if we do find ourselves lost and not knowing which way to turn, we just need to open our compass —the Bible—and get the direction we need. After all, the Word is a lamp to our feet and a light to our path. (See Psalm 119.)

Totally Free

There's a blessing when you battle for your family. When you fight for your family in the name of God, He is going to give you the victory. But God's victory is total: He gives a holistic recovery. God doesn't just save your soul and then leave you hungry. He doesn't just feed you and not put a roof over your head. God doesn't just give you housing and not give you transportation. God won't just give you transportation and not give you friends. God won't just give you friends and not give you truth in His Word. It is a holistic deliverance! He delivers you totally!

The text says that when Abram recovered all the goods, he took back his nephew, his nephew's wife, and all the other folk. But I'm still trying to figure out where he took them back to. I don't believe he took them back to Sodom. Why deliver somebody and then take them back to the place where they lost their freedom? God isn't going to set us free and put us right back in the place where we lost it all—lost our family, lost our friends, lost our community. We can't go back to Sodom. Maybe you don't know that Sodom was the nastiest place in the Bible. Do your own research. Abram didn't take them back to where they lost it all. Yet, in the next chapter, the king of Sodom reappeared. Even if we don't go back to the place, people from the place will come to find us. And I'm not talking about a mere resident of Sodom. It was the *King* of Nasty who showed up, trying to pull Lot back into the same nasty situation he had come out of. But if we keep walking in the deliverance God has given us, we will be blessed.

In Indiana recently, a woman got rearrested. She had broken out of jail thirty-five years ago. She was in prison then for killing her husband, but she said she didn't do it, and said that's why she broke out. She escaped from her guards, climbed over barbed wire, got out of bondage, and disappeared for thirty-five years. But a new taskforce in Indiana that goes after people who have escaped from prison found the woman in Tennessee and arrested her again.

We might wonder, though, how somebody who was in bondage but escaped stayed free for so long. The taskforce said it wasn't too difficult. This woman changed her identity, cut off all ties from her previous life, and established new relationships. She had a husband, children, and grandchildren. Everybody said she was a nice lady. Let's take a lesson from her. If God has set us free, we stay free by changing our identity, cutting off all ties to our previous life, and establishing new relationships. The places I used to go, I don't go anymore. The people I used to hang with, I don't hang with anymore. The things I used to do, I don't do anymore. And I've got new relationships with my brothers and sisters in Christ Jesus. God is my Father; Jesus, my Brother; the Holy Spirit my Comforter and Sanctifier.

Our Father is eager for us to fight to get our families back. If we listen to Him and obey Him, He will provide us with the training, the equipping, and the enabling to win our families back. The enemy won't just let them go; we've got to go get them. But we are not alone. There are brothers and sisters also born into the household of faith who will organize with us, and we can pull together to help set other people free. Once they are free, the Holy Spirit can empower them, as He does us, to walk in that freedom. No matter how hard the fight, or how dark the circumstances in which we are fighting, we know already that we are on the winning side. We provide the willingness to be used, and God equips us with all we need to be victorious.

VI

I Want My Groove Back

¹Now for the matters you wrote about: It is good for a man not to marry. ²But since there is so much immorality, each man should have his own wife, and each woman her own husband. ³The husband should fulfill his marital duty to his wife, and likewise the wife to her husband. ⁴The wife's body does not belong to her alone but also to her husband. In the same way, the husband's body does not belong to him alone but also to his wife. ⁵Do not deprive each other except by mutual consent and for a time, so that you may devote yourselves to prayer. Then come together again so that Satan will not tempt you because of your lack of self-control. ⁶I say this as a concession, not as a command. ⁷I wish that all men were as I am. But each man has his own gift from God; one has this gift, another has that.

⁸Now to the unmarried and the widows I say: It is good for them to stay unmarried, as I am. ⁹But if they cannot control themselves, they should marry, for it is better to marry than to burn with passion.

¹⁰To the married I give this command (not I, but the Lord): A wife must not separate from her husband.

¹¹But if she does, she must remain unmarried or else be reconciled to her husband. And a husband must not divorce his wife.

¹²To the rest I say this (I, not the Lord): If any brother has a wife who is not a believer and she is willing to live with him, he must not divorce her. ¹³And if a woman has a husband who is not a believer and he is willing to live with her, she must not divorce him. ¹⁴For the unbelieving husband has been sanctified through his wife, and the unbelieving wife has been sanctified through her believing husband. Otherwise your children would be unclean, but as it is, they are holy. ¹⁵But if the unbeliever leaves, let him do so. A believing man or woman is not bound in such circumstances; God has called us to live in peace. ¹⁶How do you know, wife, whether you will save your husband? Or, how do you know, husband, whether you will save your wife?

(I Corinthians 7:1-16)

A friend of mine who is single called me one day to tell me that some woman had sent a picture of herself to his cell phone. He was really happy, telling me how fine she was, that she was gorgeous, and how good he felt having her picture in his cell phone. A few days later when we were talking, he complained, "Man, I can't figure out how to delete this woman out of my cell phone." He said, "Every time I flip my phone open, she's right there, so no matter who I'm talking to, every conversation I have is colored by her image." By now, she's not only in his cell phone, but she has gotten into his head as well. He continually sees her picture, and she stays in his mind because he has an image of her that he cannot delete.

A few weeks later when we were talking, I remembered this situation and asked him, "Did you ever get that woman's picture out of your phone?" He said, "Yes, I finally got it out, and I'm glad. It was driving me crazy." I asked him how he was finally able to get rid of it. He explained, "Well, either after thirty days it was just automatically deleted, or it could be that when someone else sent a picture to my cell phone, the new picture displaced that one." Whichever it was, she's gone.

Time to Say Bye-Bye

There are times when we all realize that we have someone we need to delete out of our lives. You may be facing that right now. You have been connected with someone in some kind of way. Even though you know the relationship is not of God, you have become so emotionally entangled with him or her that you don't know how to delete the person. What's really bad is that this man or woman has so gotten into your head that every time you try to have a conversation—no matter who it's with—there he is, or there she is.

I want to tell you how to delete this person so that you can go on with your life as God intended. The first thing you need to know is that it's going to take time. When you get emotionally entangled with somebody, even if it's somebody you're not supposed to be with, it takes time to get that person out of your spirit, your mindset, and your head. I've been told that when you get entangled with somebody and then break off the relationship, it takes at least twelve months to get that person out of your spirit. But if you let the person come back and have significant contact again (whatever that might mean to you), your twelve months start all over again. So you need to give yourself time to heal.

The second thing you need is to get somebody else in that picture in your mind. You need to have another picture to come in so that the first image will leave. The person whom I suggest you choose is Jesus. When you get Jesus, He'll begin to color your conversations and your relationships; then, everything is going to be all right.

What About Today?

In our text, the church at Corinth has gotten in touch with the apostle Paul. They have been trying to figure out, as Christians, how they are supposed to relate to one another. They have written Paul a letter asking him how single Christians are supposed to handle their personal and interpersonal relationships. They also ask about Christians who are married: when things are not going well for a married Christian couple, how do they handle that? Is it okay to separate or get a divorce? The third situation they ask him about involves the Christian who is married to a non-Christian. Is it okay for the Christian to leave that relationship?

Paul writes back to them, and we catch his responses in chapter 7. Basically, he says to the single people that they are to stay single, and to the married people that they are to remain married, even if one of the partners is not a Christian. This may not be a popular line of thinking today and, if truth be told, it probably wasn't what the people of Corinth wanted to hear, either. But if you are a Christian and you want to get your groove back, you need to follow what the Word of God has to say.

Now whenever you are reading scripture, you have to deal with it in its biblical, historical, and cultural context. When Paul was writing to the believers of the first century, this was a group of people who believed, as Paul did, that Jesus was going to return at any moment. When they talked about the second coming of Christ, they thought He was coming back at any time. This was so much the case that believers in Thessalonica had quit their jobs. They were thinking, "Why do we need jobs? Jesus is going to come back soon." Paul had to tell them that if they didn't work, they wouldn't eat.

So, even as Paul is talking here to single people and married couples, he is speaking from their perception that they were not living in the first century, but the *last* century. He, too, thought Jesus was coming back any day, so to a single person, he advised, "Just stay single. Jesus will be here soon, so don't get tangled up in a relationship that takes your time and energy away from the things of God. It may not be easy, but just stay as you are and serve God with all your heart." To the married people, he was saying, "Just hang in there. No matter what you're going through, it won't be long. Jesus will be back shortly; just wait a few more days."

Paul wanted the people to understand that there is no relationship that should get in the way of their relationship with God—and that holds true in any century. The kingdom of God has to take priority, so we have to be sure never to let anyone, no matter who it is, come between us and our relationship with Jesus Christ. Whether we're married or single, we cannot allow our relationships to stand in the way of what we have with God.

So then, we wonder, "What if Paul had known it would be over two thousand years before Jesus came back?" Twenty centuries have now passed, and Jesus still has not returned. Would Paul still have said to the same single person, "It's going to be twenty centuries, but just stay single," or to the married person, "Well, it's going to be a while, but don't change anything"? These are questions we need to deal with as we respond to the challenges presented today.

A Word to Singles

One thing in this matter is clear: regardless of what time period we're in, no matter what century, the *principles* are the same. Since that is the case, why would Paul tell a single person to stay single? It's because a single person has the opportunity to give undivided attention to Jesus. If you are single, you can focus on Jesus without having to divide your time and attention as married people do.

Just this week, I was in Chicago to preach for two nights. The church really wanted me to stay longer than that, but I couldn't because I needed to get back to my family. Even though I was there doing what God has called me to do, I also have a wife and children to be concerned about. My calling into ministry does not negate my responsibilities toward my family, so I am not free to be away from them whenever an opportunity arises for me to preach. Nor would I *want* to be away from them for extended periods.

God has first place in my life and in the lives of my wife and children, but we do also love one another and have responsibilities and commitments toward one another. When you're single, you don't have to divide your time like that. I understand that you don't have *more* time when you're single. Some married folk think that single people have nothing to do when they are not at work—that they have no responsibilities and no real commitments. Now, I know that is not true. We all have only twenty-four hours in a day and, whether we're single or married, there are people, situations, and needs constantly demanding our attention. But the one thing that most single people have more than married couples is *flexibility* in their time, more *options* in the use of their time. I would encourage you to use this time as a special gift from God. Give your undivided service to the kingdom of God and your undivided devotion to God. You may not have this opportunity in the future, so don't waste it. That's why Paul says if you're single, stay single; don't be in a hurry to tie yourself to other obligations and distractions.

Now, the problem with many of us, especially those of us who married young, is that we think that being single is some kind of a sickness, that it carries some sort of shame with it. If you're single, you've probably encountered someone who has asked you, "Are you *still* single?" And they say it as though you have some kind of a disease that you can't get rid of: "You're not married *yet*? Well, I'm sorry." You probably hate to go to family reunions, don't you? You dread hearing, "You aren't bringing anybody?" "How come you're still single?" "Don't you know your biological clock is ticking?" Friend, when you are single, saved, sanctified, and satisfied, there is no shame. You don't have a sickness, and being married isn't going to cure you.

It is in this time of being single that you need to work on your spirituality. Stop getting upset because of who is not in your life or who is or is not trying to get with you. This is a special time for you to draw as close to God as you possibly can. Also, it is the time for you to work on yourself. While you are single, you need to pursue your education, acquire your training, improve your mind, work on your body, develop a healthy self-image, establish your career, and get your finances together. Why? Because this is the best time you will ever have to do those things. Don't get caught up in the fallacy that once you are married, everything will be better or easier: "*then* I can pursue the job I really want," "*then* I can go back to school," "*then* I'll have the money I need," or "*then* I'll start taking care of myself." It doesn't work like that!

I've had people tell me they want to get married, and when I ask why, they say, "Because then I will have somebody to complete me." Let me speak honestly with you. If you are incomplete while you are single, you are still going to be incomplete when you get married. You don't marry somebody to complete you, as though you are just half a person looking for another half-person. If you think two half-people can make a whole marriage, you are wrong. That's not going to happen. You have to be complete on your own. Paul says that the two shall become one: one whole person marries another whole person, and they have one whole marriage. Don't think that someone else can complete you, especially when Colossians 2:10 (KJV) tells us that our completion is in Christ, not in another human being: ". . .and ye are complete in Him, which is the head of all principality and power." So, while you are single, work on your spirituality, work on yourself, and work on your service to God.

Hot and Holy

Paul's advice to singles was to remain unmarried so that they might please the Lord. But here's the issue. In the text for this chapter, Paul says he wishes that single people would remain single, but not everybody can handle being single. Some people have the gift of celibacy, and some don't. So Paul says it's better for a person to marry than to burn with passion. Many of us are too hot to stay single.

Dr. Theron Williams pointed something out to me that I hadn't noticed before: it is possible to be hot and holy at the same time. In the first chapter, it says Paul is writing to the holy ones in Corinth.

151

Then, in this passage, he says to the same people, *the holy ones in Corinth*, it is better to marry than to burn with passion. Some of the holy ones were experiencing the heat of passion. Sexual passion is normal; it's a sign of a healthy body. Some people act like those who have this burning passion within them are sinful—that if they were close enough to God, they wouldn't be feeling that way. That just isn't true! It is possible to be hot and holy at the same time.

It's important for us to know that, because sometimes our expectations are skewed. I've had a sister come to me who told me she had found a good man; he loved God, was active in the church, treated her well, and had a lot of great qualities. But she broke up with him because he was sexually attracted to her. Now there's something wrong with that kind of thinking: a woman should be concerned when a man who says he loves her is *not* sexually attracted to her. It is possible to be hot and holy at the same time! Now, the key is to not let that passion lead to sin. You've got to stay holy in the midst of a heated situation. That's why Paul says it's better to marry than to burn.

Now some saint reading this book may be thinking, "I don't know why he's even bringing all this up. When I got saved and filled with the Spirit, God just took that desire away from me. Jesus just keeps me, and I don't even get hot like that anymore." That reminds me of a Mama Sadie, who taught little kids in Sunday school for years. She used to tell them every Sunday, "Mama Sadie doesn't need anybody but Jesus. It's just me and Jesus." Every Sunday she would tell the kids the same thing: "Mama Sadie doesn't need anybody but Jesus. It's just Mama Sadie and Jesus. Jesus is all I need." Sunday after Sunday, she would testify to the children that it was just her and Jesus.

But one Sunday, the kids were on their way to Sunday school early that day. As they passed by Mama Sadie's house, they saw a man jumping out the back window with his shoes in his hand. When they got to Sunday school, before Mama Sadie could talk, they said to her, "Mama Sadie, we saw Jesus jumping out your back window this morning." You can be hot and holy! But here's what you don't want to happen. You don't want somebody who's hot but can't handle it to distract you from your holiness. And it's not just single people who need to be careful.

Sometimes when I'm on my way home after a long, hard day, I'll call Sharon and tell her I'm on my way home and ask her to start running a bath for me. Now when Sharon runs bath water, it's so hot you could cook in it. It's hot! Now it doesn't bother her because she has a higher tolerance for heat than I do, but I can't take it. Two partners can experience the same degree of heat. One of you can handle it, but the other can't. You cannot let someone who can't handle their hotness stand in the way of your holiness.

When you are passionate, you have to make sure your passion has some direction. A Christian cannot have misdirected passion. In Song of Solomon 1:2, the woman says she wants her lover to kiss her with the kisses of his mouth. She is passionate, she's hot, but she is not expressing that passion to everybody.

She is speaking only to the particular person whom God has given to her. I believe it was Janet Jackson who sang, "I don't want to get so lonely that I let anybody hold me." You see, your passion has to have direction so that when you're hot, you aren't trying to get with everybody.

Now you may be saying, "But wait a minute. I'm a single Christian and I'm hot and holy, but I'm having trouble finding a man, or trouble finding a woman. So how do I deal with that? I'm willing to marry rather than burn, but I don't have anyone to marry—no matter how much I'm burning. How do I handle it if I'm hot and holy, but I can't find a good man or a good woman?" I think it's impossible for you not to find a good mate if you are truly hot and holy. Recently on the television news, we were seeing scenes from wildfires that were occurring in California. The fires got so hot that people from all over the country were showing up—firefighters, policemen, EMTs, paramedics, doctors, and psychiatrists. They came in helicopters, planes, cars, and on motorcycles because of the fire. If you are truly on fire, you will find someone showing up.

But keep in mind that if the *only* reason you decide to get married is because you are hot, you are going to have issues. You need to be sure you are marrying someone because you love that person, you worship the same God, you share the same values, you are walking in the same direction, and you want to spend the rest of your lives together. If you marry someone only because you're hot, you're going to have problems. Beginning in verse 10, Paul starts talking about problems in marriage that can lead to separation and divorce. There are times, if you aren't careful, that you will get married for the wrong reasons, and eventually your marriage will fall apart.

A Message to Married Folk

Watch what Paul says to those who are married. If you are married, his word to you, in any century, is: stay married. You may be protesting, "But you don't know how hard it is. You don't know how difficult my life is. You don't know what I'm going through."

Most divorces in America occur during the first four years of marriage. Within four years of saying, "I do," the couple is ready to say, "I don't anymore." The wife is ready to delete her husband from her life, or the husband is ready to delete his wife. It was interesting to me that my friend who received the woman's picture on his cell phone wasn't troubled when he received it. Trying to delete it, however, was driving him crazy. How does somebody go from contentment to crazy in a few days?

When you have marital problems, the answer to your problems is not divorce. Somebody asked me just recently what I think about divorce. I think the same way God does about divorce. The Bible says that God hates divorce. *He hates it.* Now He does make concessions for certain people to get divorced, such as a situation involving adultery. If one of the mates is unfaithful, the other can seek a divorce. That person doesn't *have* to get a divorce because

God doesn't *command* it. He merely *allows* it if the partner feels he or she cannot work things out. God can, however, even restore a marriage that has suffered from infidelity.

The second concession God makes regarding divorce is abandonment. You'll see that in 1 Corinthians 7:15. If an unbelieving spouse decides to leave, Paul says, "Let him/her go." He adds, "God has called us to live in peace." If someone doesn't want to live with you, you don't want to live with them. Let the person go, and let your life be at peace. If you are abandoned, you are free to get on with your life.

There is a third concession that Paul doesn't mention, but I'm going to name it here: abuse. Someone reading this book may know that your life is on the line right now because somebody in your own house is trying to hurt you. You do not have to live in an abusive situation; you do not have to wait for your spouse to kill you. God will get no glory from having you die at the hands of an abuser. God *delivers* people from hell; He doesn't consign us to stay there.

It's interesting how some people put up with unfaithfulness, abandonment, or abuse for years, even though God has offered a way out. Yet others, at the first sign of difficulty in a marriage, are ready to call it quits. For this latter group, the answer to your marital problems is not divorce: it's meeting their spouse's needs. Real love is not a feeling that you feel that you've never felt before. You may say, "I *love* him," or "I *love* her," but how do you know? "Because it's a feeling I feel that I've never felt before," you reply. But that feeling could just be indigestion.

Dr. A. Louis Patterson, Jr. says that real love is not a feeling; it's an act of your will. You *will* to love somebody. Real love is a minimum of emotion and a maximum of evaluating and meeting needs. When you operate based on feelings, you'll find your "love" constantly fluctuating. Sometimes you feel like it, and sometimes you don't. You don't stay married because of an emotional tie; you *will* to love your spouse. If you really love someone, you evaluate that person's need and do whatever it takes to meet it, even when it requires an act of self-sacrifice, even when you don't feel like doing it. That's how you can tell if what you feel for someone is genuine love. Have you evaluated that person's need? Have you gone out of your way to meet that need? Have you sacrificed to make it happen, even when you didn't feel like doing it?

That's also how you can tell if somebody really loves you. It's not just because the person says, "I love you." Words are cheap. Has that person evaluated your need? Is that person attempting to meet that need, even when he or she doesn't feel like doing it? Meeting your partner's need is the key to getting your marriage back on track, the key to getting your groove back.

Meeting Each Other's Needs

What happens too often in marriage, however, is that you have a husband doing for a wife what he really wants her to do for him, or you have a wife doing for her husband what she really wants him to do for her. So you think you are meeting your spouse's needs, but you really aren't doing that at all. Instead, you're trying to meet your *own* needs. Because men and women have different needs, you can't figure out what you want and do that for your spouse. You have to figure out what your husband or wife actually wants. You could spend two or three years or more doing things for your spouse and still never meet his or her needs. You may feel like you're very self-sacrificing and truly putting yourself out to do those things, but if it isn't really what that person *needs*, you're just wasting your time. So you are frustrated because your spouse isn't responding, and your mate is frustrated because his or her needs aren't being met.

So how do you deal with that? In my earlier book, *Song of Solomon: Love, Sex and Relationships*, there is a chapter entitled "Show Me How to Love You." You don't have to waste time trying to *guess* what your partner wants or needs—just ask! "What is it that you want? What is it that you need for me to do for you?" But be prepared, because you probably aren't going to get the answer you expected. Your needs are different from your spouse's needs, so you're not going to hear the same answer that you would give if you were asked that question. First Corinthians 7:3 says that a husband ought to give his wife what she is due; likewise, the wife should give her husband his due. When you get married, you've got to give your spouse what he or she needs.

Her Needs

Dr. Willard F. Harley, Jr., a noted psychologist and author who specializes in marriage counseling, outlined in his book *His Needs, Her Needs: Building An Affair-proof Marriage*, the unique needs of wives and husbands. Husband, your wife needs attention and affection from you; she needs for you to focus in on her. She wants to know that she is the most important person in your life. She needs to be complimented *by you*. It doesn't matter if men at her job or in other places compliment her: she wants to hear it from you. She gets compliments all the time from men at her workplace: "I hope your husband knows how lucky he is, because you're so fine." She gets them walking down the street: "Hey, girl! I know your husband can't handle that. You need a real man." She gets them at church: "I know your husband realizes how God has blessed him to have found a wife like you." But then she goes home and can't get any love, attention, affection, and compliments from him.

Your wife also needs to know that you are fully committed to your family. What have you done recently to assure her that your family is a priority in your life? Moreover, a wife needs to know that her husband will provide financially for the family. A wife can't handle it when her husband is lying around the house doing nothing when the bills are coming due. A wife also needs openness and honesty. You see, brother, you cannot be intimate with somebody to whom you're lying. You can have sex, but you can't have closeness and intimacy if you are lying to your wife. Communicate with your wife. Find out what her needs are, and work to meet them.

A few days ago, I was watching highlights on ESPN. They were showing the field at a Washington state high school football game before the game actually started. The band was playing, the crowd was cheering, and there was a large paper banner with the name and logo of the team stretched out, ready for the home team to come out and run through it as they came onto the field. But just as the team was coming out, running full speed toward the back of the banner, ready to burst through it and onto the field, a cheerleader ran in front of the banner to make an adjustment, and she got tackled by the team. The men were running over someone who was there to support them, somebody who was there cheering for them. Of course, the reason they ran over her was because they couldn't see her. And, brother, you need to make sure you aren't running over the one supporting you because you aren't seeing her the way you're supposed to see her.

His Needs

Wife, you need to give your husband what is due him. You've got to be your husband's biggest cheerleader. Even when no one else is cheering for him, you need to cheer for him. You need to meet his needs. Don't talk about needing a divorce; that's not the answer to your marital problems. The answer to your problems involves meeting his needs. You may protest, "But I've been doing this, and that, and this and ...." But is that meeting his needs? It's cool that you're sending him cards, letters, cologne, and sweet little notes. But those are things *you* want; that's not what will meet *his* needs. Brothers have different needs from you. One of the things he needs is an attractive wife. What I mean by that is not some fake, phony, false beauty contestant; a brother just wants his wife to look something like the woman he married. When he married you, he liked you the way you were. Some women, however, may not resemble very much the persons they were when they got married. Now, if I've hit a nerve with you personally, you can either get mad at me and slam down the book, or you can take it to heart and begin to meet your husband's needs. It's your choice.

A brother also needs respect and honor, especially in his own home. A man needs for his home to be his castle. A man needs admiration, and he particularly needs it from his wife. Sisters, your man has an ego. You can either stress over it or stroke it, but the ego isn't going anywhere. Notice that Ephesians 5 says for husbands to love their wives, but it doesn't instruct wives to love their husbands. The reason is that generally, women automatically love their husbands. But the Bible instructs wives to reverence and respect their husbands because that doesn't happen automatically. And a brother needs respect, especially in his own home from his own wife.

Another thing a brother needs is peace and quiet. The answer isn't divorce; the answer is to get peace and quiet in your home. Solomon, the wisest man ever, said in Proverbs 17:1 that he would rather have a dry morsel in quietness than have a great feast in a house that has strife; and in Proverbs 25:24, he said that it's better to live on a rooftop than in a house with a quarrelsome wife. A man cannot take a nagging wife. You may object, "But I've got to tell him this. If he'd do what he's supposed to, I wouldn't have to nag him. It isn't like you think. Our situation is different. I *have* to keep on my husband to get anything done...." That's what I'm talking about; he can't take that! When you are doing that, he can't even hear you. He may be standing right in front of you, but if you go off like that, his eyes will glaze over, his ears will stop up, and he won't have any idea what you are saying. To him, you will sound like Charlie Brown's teacher: "Wha, wa, wa, wha, wa. Wha, wa. wa, and wa, wa, wa....."

The Importance of Sex

In verse 3, it says that husbands and wives have to perform their marital duty to each other because their bodies belong to each other, not to themselves. If you withhold your body from your husband or if you refuse to have sex with your wife, you leave room for the devil to come in. The only time the Bible suggests a couple might want to refrain from having sexual relations is if they are spending a period of time earnestly praying and seeking God. Even then, both partners must be in total agreement, and it is not to be for a long period of time. Most of the time, you need to be praying *and* having sex. Don't get so spiritual that you think you're more holy because

162

you're refraining from sex. God intends for married couples to experience the intimacy that comes through sexual intercourse. You cannot deprive your mate of your body and still expect for your marriage to remain healthy.

In fact, Dr. Harley also states that sex is a husband's number one need. A wife's primary need is affection; a husband's main need is sex. What's crazy is that so often there's a husband trying to give sex to his wife, and a wife trying to give affection to her husband. You need to switch that up. Brother, you need to set the environment for affection, and, sister, you need to bring the sex. If you don't do that, you leave room for the devil to come in. When a brother gets married, he is looking forward to having sex, sex, and more sex. When he stood at the altar during the wedding and said, "Yes, I take her... yes, I forsake all others...," he was envisioning a continual supply of sex. But if he doesn't get any, he feels like he's been cheated, and, whether he says it or not, he's thinking about his wife, "I gave up everybody else for you, and now you won't meet the number one need that I have." This leaves room for the enemy to come in.

When I first started doing research on this subject a few years ago, I read that studies indicate (in general) men think about sex every fifteen minutes, and women think about sex once a week. I can't fathom that. How can a person think about sex only one time a week?! Now, I've read that some studies show that men think about sex every *ten* minutes. If that's true, it means that even when a brother is sitting in church, the pastor is going to lose his attention at least four times in every forty-minute sermon! Sisters, you need to understand that. If you bring a forced abstinence into your marriage, your effort to control your husband is going to backfire. You think that because you are both Christians and God has said you can only have sex within the confines of marriage, you can control your husband by giving him sex when he's pleasing you and withholding it from him when you're upset about something. You have placed him on a reward-and-punishment system. But, sister, you are dealing with a man's number one need: he has a sexual appetite. You can't continually withhold what your husband needs, what he is hungry for, without leaving room for the enemy to come in.

My wife, by her choice, is a full-time home-maker, and she's great at it. She lovingly provides me and our children with a home that is a refuge, a place of comfort, a place we look forward to coming to after we've spent some time in a world that is often harsh, impersonal, and difficult. One of the things she does is prepare delicious meals for us. Now, if I sit down to one of my wife's four-course meals, which she even tops off with some dessert, I am full. So, when I leave our home and drive down to the church for a meeting that night, I'm no longer hungry. It doesn't matter that I pass by McDonald's, Steak 'n Shake, P.F. Chang's, Cracker Barrel, and all those other restaurants. Even if I like them and they would normally tempt me to stop, I'm not stopping. Why? Because I'm full: I just ate at home. Sisters, if you want your husband to drive by the alternatives he encounters each day without being tempted, you need to feed him at home.

As my friend, Dr. Frederick Haynes, III, senior pastor of Friendship-West Baptist Church in Dallas, points out, another challenge in marriage is that "too many people get married based on an *i*deal. But after a while, you find your marriage is turning into an *or*deal. You begin to feel that you're getting a *raw* deal, and may begin looking for a *new* deal." But I'm trying to tell you that the answer to having a healthy, growing, satisfying marriage is for both the husband and wife to resolve to meet the needs of the other.

In Summary

To sum up what Paul has said, if you're single, stay single. Be satisfied with who you are in God, and develop yourself in the Lord. Give your time, energy, and attention to Him. But if you're so hot you can't handle being celibate, you need to get married. Be sure, however, that you marry a Christian; it is never right for a Christian to marry an unbeliever. It is never right for a Christian to be unequally yoked with a non-Christian.

In September 2007, crocodile hunter Steve Irwin died when a stingray pierced his heart with its tail. Just a month later, an eighty-one-year-old man got a stingray tail through *his* heart and lived. The man was in a boat, and the stingray literally jumped out of the water right into the man's lap. Even though the stingray stuck his tail into the man's heart, he lived. Now, first of all, there is a warning in that story about being careful who you allow to get in your lap. But this old man was just minding his own business, not looking for a stingray, when one came and jumped right into his lap. However, you still have to be wary of things that you know can sting you. But this story also raises the question, how is it that the younger and very healthy Steve Irwin died when a stingray put its tail through his heart, yet the old man had the same thing happen to him, and he lived? The difference is that Steve Irwin himself took the tail out and bled to death, but James Bertakis let the doctor take it out and lived. There is a lesson there for us. If we have to get a tail out of our hearts, we need to let the Great Physician do it.

Now, if you are already married, stay married by meeting the needs of your spouse. If you are married to an unbeliever, the Word tells you to be faithful to your spouse. Don't use the fact that your husband or wife is not a Christian as an excuse for infidelity. You may be feeling that your marriage is getting in the way of your ministry; your relationship with your spouse is getting between you and your relationship with your God; your companion is getting in the way of your conversion; or your family is getting in the way of your faith. When you were first married, perhaps neither of you were Christians; neither of you cared about the things of God. But then you came to know Christ personally so now you want to worship and serve Him, but your still-unsaved spouse is proving to be a hindrance to you. But it should never be the case that the relationship with your spouse is hindering your relationship with

God; instead, your relationship with God should be *improving* your relationship with your spouse. Paul says if your spouse is willing to stay with you, you need to stay with him or her because when you start demonstrating Christianity in front of your spouse, it should have a positive impact upon his or her life. You can't change your spouse, but God can. The God in you should be so attractive that your life will draw your mate to Christ. God is able to step into a messed-up situation and turn it completely around, but you've got to trust Him.

From Disappointment to Joy

I want to close this chapter the same way I opened it—by speaking to singles. A few years ago, I was in Miami, Florida, waiting in the lobby of a four-star resort for the valet to retrieve my rental car so that I could go to South Beach for dinner. After an excessively long delay, the valet came *walking* up to me and told me the car had a flat. Already late and feeling perturbed because the tire wasn't flat when I drove the car into the hotel a couple hours earlier, but not wanting to take any longer than necessary, I told him to give me the keys and I would change the tire, rather than having to wait for an auto service to come and fix it. I got the keys to the car, opened up the trunk, took out the jack, took off the lug nuts, and then removed the flat tire. But when I tried to put on the spare tire, it didn't fit! Now I was really upset. My tire was flat, my car was jacked up, I was trying to get to my destination, and I was running late.

I realized I could not get to my destination in that car under the present circumstances. I could either stay where I was with a jacked-up situation that didn't fit, or I could get on the phone and call the one who was able to provide what I needed. So I called the rental company. They were apologetic about my situation, told me just to stay put, and said they would be there as soon as possible to fix my situation. So I waited patiently and they did come a little while later, but they didn't come and fix the flat so I could drive *that* car. Instead, they brought me a sweet, brand-new, late-model Mustang convertible to replace it! I jumped into my new ride and made it to my destination. The old ride couldn't get me there, but I waited patiently and a new one showed up and got me where I needed to go. If you are single and in a relationship that has gone flat and is jacked up because it was a bad fit, you've got to let it go. Then call upon God, wait patiently, and He will bring a new relationship that is sweeter and better than the one you were trying to make work. And with that new relationship, you will be able to get where you need to go.

VII

I Want My Joy Back

¹Have mercy on me, O God, according to your unfailing love; according to your great compassion blot out my transgressions. ² Wash away all my iniquity and cleanse me from my sin. ³For I know my transgressions, and my sin is always before me. ⁴Against you, you only, have I sinned and done what is evil in your sight, so that you are proved right when you speak and justified when you judge.

⁵Surely I was sinful at birth, sinful from the time my mother conceived me. ⁶Surely you desire truth in the inner parts; you teach me wisdom in the inmost place. ⁷Cleanse me with hyssop, and I will be clean; wash me, and I will be whiter than snow. ⁸Let me hear joy and gladness; let the bones you have crushed rejoice. ⁹Hide your face from my sins and blot out all my iniquity.

¹⁰Create in me a pure heart, O God, and renew a steadfast spirit within me. ¹¹Do not cast me from your presence or take your Holy Spirit from me. ¹²Restore to me the joy of your salvation and grant me a willing spirit, to sustain me. ¹³Then I will teach transgressors your ways, and sinners will turn back to you. ¹⁴Save

me from bloodguilt, O God, the God who saves me, and my tongue will sing of your righteousness. [15]O Lord, open my lips, and my mouth will declare your praise.

[16]You do not delight in sacrifice, or I would bring it; you do not take pleasure in burnt offerings. [17]The sacrifices of God are a broken spirit; a broken and contrite heart, O God, you will not despise.

[18]In your good pleasure make Zion prosper; build up the walls of Jerusalem. [19]Then there will be righteous sacrifices, whole burnt offerings to delight you; then bulls will be offered on your altar.

(Psalm 51)

When my second son Jordan was much younger, he came in one day while I was sitting in my bedroom, channel surfing on the TV. Noticing that a hockey game was on at that moment, he asked, "Daddy, who's winning?" To tell you the truth, I don't know a whole lot about hockey. I do appreciate that the players are professional athletes who have made it to a certain level with discipline and success, but I just haven't followed the sport. I replied to Jordan, "I don't know, son. I just turned it on, and they haven't shown the score. I don't know who is winning." But Jordan pointed at one of the teams and said, "They must be winning, because they are excited and jumping up and down." Even though he had just walked in, knew very little about the game, and the score hadn't been flashed on the screen yet, he could look at the demeanor of the teams and tell who was on the winning side.

Behaving Like Winners

Let me ask you, if somebody who doesn't know Jesus walked into your church on a Sunday morning, would that person be able to tell that your church is on the winning team? I'm suggesting that one of the ways people will be able to tell who is on *God's* winning team is based upon our own demeanor and disposition. When we walk around looking or acting mean, evil, and hard to get along with, always down, always depressed, always disillusioned, folk can't tell we're on the winning team. We've got to get more enthusiastic and more excited about the things of God. We've got to get back to the place where we have joy with God. What is it that has robbed us of our joy?

The Bible tells us to "rejoice, and again I say rejoice," but not many of us are rejoicing. The Bible tells us to "be of good cheer" because Jesus has already overcome the world, but very few of us are of good cheer. There was a time that we used to have joy. We used to be enthused about God. There was a time when other folk could look at our lives and know that we were on the winning team, but now…? That's why some of us can't win family members, friends, and coworkers to Christ. Who wants to serve a God whose followers are always down and depressed? My mentor says that people come to church initially because they're invited, but they come back because they like it.

There ought to be a certain amount of joy when we come into the house of God. But I believe there are joy-takers and joy-breakers, and I wonder what it is that's been taking our joy. I wonder what it is that has so many of us walking around as though we're on a losing team. To learn what it is, look at Psalm 51. David is expressing himself—that he has lost his joy. This is the same David who says elsewhere, "I will bless the Lord at all times"; the same David who says, "Let everything that hath breath praise the Lord"; the same David who says, "Come into His presence with thanksgiving and into His courts with praise"; the same David who boasted and bragged about the joy he experienced with God. But now it's gone. I wonder what it was that took his joy.

Sin Displaces Our Joy

What is it that removes joy from our lives? With David, it was sexual sin. He wrote Psalm 51 after his experience with Bathsheba. He had slept with a married woman, and she became pregnant. Today, we live in a sex-crazed society. Casual sexual affairs, adultery, fornication, and pornography are running rampant in our society. There is no other way to put it except to say that we are sex-*crazed*. We still end up in one-night stands even though we know that when we sleep with somebody, we're not just sleeping with that person, but with everyone that person has ever slept with; we sleep with that person's sexual history. We still have casual sexual affairs even though we know that sexually transmitted diseases are on the rise; and we seem to think that because we can have "protected sex" and have access to effective birth control methods that those somehow negate the moral and spiritual dimensions of sexuality.

Everywhere you turn there is sexual innuendo or blatant sexual activity. You can hardly watch a movie or a music video without seeing some type of pornography. Some people reading this will think I'm an old fogy, antiquated and outdated. No, I'm just biblical. I still believe what the Bible says—that the bed inside of marriage is undefiled; it's clean, holy, and wholesome. But outside of marriage, it's dirty, defiled, and nasty. It doesn't matter whether it's fornication, adultery or pornography; it is all outside the will of God. These sexual sins are robbing us of our joy.

But for those of us who have a clean conscience when it comes to adultery or fornication, those of us who have not been engaging in sexual sins, we need to know that adultery was not the only sin David committed. Another thing robbing him of his joy was secret sins. David found himself in a big mess and only made it worse by trying to get out of it. There he was, sleeping with another man's wife, and after he got her pregnant, he decided he would try to hide his sin rather than confess that he had done wrong. So he usurped his kingly authority that was given to him by God and arranged to have Bathsheba's husband put on the frontlines of battle so that he would be killed. After her husband was gone, David married Bathsheba, thinking everything was hidden. He thought he had gotten away with his sins.

But secrets will mess us up. From God's perspective, there are no secret sins. Hidden sins on earth are open scandals in heaven. You can pull all the shades, lock all the doors, turn out all the lights, or hide in a back alley, but God sees all and He knows all. Now, I understand that what I'm saying here is not a popular twenty-first century message. To become a popular author, I'm supposed to make you feel good, promise you a raise and a promotion, and tell you that you are going to be wealthy and happy. That may happen to you, but it is just as likely that you are among those who have lost their joy. Sin is a joy-taker and a joy-breaker. When we try to hide our sins, we lose the joy and enthusiasm we used to have with God. God knows all that we've done, and so do we, no matter how hard we try to forget.

Confession Restores Joy

God loved David too much to let him off the hook. That's why he sent the prophet Nathan to David to confront him with the fact that he had usurped his authority as king, slept with another man's wife, murdered a man to try to hide his adultery, and had never confessed his sins. What I've discovered is that when we don't confess our sin on our own, God will uncover it.

God gives us guilt for a particular reason. Even if we are Christians—we have a right relationship with God through His Son Jesus Christ—and then we sin, there is a strong sense of guilt that is produced inside of us. Even if nobody else saw us, there is still an inner guilt, a work of our conscience that lets us know we have done something that has come between us and our fellowship with God. Even if we consciously try to ignore it, we toss and turn at night, knowing that something just isn't right. Why does that happen? Because God will not let us rest until we confess.

If we won't confess on our own, God will pull back the covers on our secret sin. Ephesians 5:13 even talks about how that which is done in the dark is going to be revealed in the light. And when God reveals these secret sins, He's not doing it to try to hurt you or beat you down, but to restore your fellowship with Him. God knows that most of us are not truly sorry for our sin; we're only sorry if we get caught. So God says, "I want you to confess your sin so that our fellowship can be restored, so I'm going to uncover your sin—not to hurt you, but to cause you to finally confess the sin that you never should have committed in the first place." Our sorrow should not be over the fact that we get caught, but over the fact that we got caught *up* in sin because it's such a joy-stealer.

David prays in this psalm, "Restore unto me the joy of my salvation." If secret sin removes our joy, then what can restore that joy? Some people think they can find their joy in other people. It is interesting that we even try to get joy from people whom we know are in a sorrowful situation themselves. We know these people don't have their own situation together, but we try to get them to help us get our situation together. How can somebody living in sorrow give *you* joy?

Others look for joy not in people, but in places. You've moved fifty times, thinking if you can just get to another city or another environment, you will find joy. Moves can be good, and sometimes a new location can give us a new lease on life; but a new location can't salve our consciences or restore our fellowship with God. And what we find out when we move is that we can leave other situations and people behind us, but we still have to take ourselves along. If we are not at rest within ourselves, that unrest will follow us—no matter where we go. A new location can't restore our joy.

Others look for joy in possessions. We buy one thing after another because it promises to make us happy and meet a need. We run from one store to another, one mall to another, trying to buy enough stuff to satisfy the need inside ourselves for joy. And sometimes things can bring us momentary happiness. We can feel happy when we wear a new outfit for the first time, when we invite our friends over to watch the game on our new big-screen TV, or when we roll up to work in our new car. But happiness and joy are not the same thing. Happiness is based on what is *happening*, on happenstance. So, if what is happening to me is favorable, I am happy; if what is happening to me is unfavorable, I am unhappy. Happiness, therefore, is always based on situations and circumstances.

Joy, on the other hand, is not based on something that is happening to me externally; instead, it is something I have inside of me, internally. It is a fruit of the Spirit. When we have the Holy Spirit inside and are walking in the Spirit, living by the Spirit, speaking in the Spirit, and praying in the Spirit, the Holy Spirit will give us joy. Grandma says it's a joy that the world can't give, and the world can't take away. We're not talking about happiness; we're talking about joy. And the kind of joy we're talking about will not come unless we confess our sins.

Owning Our Sins

Sin removes our joy, but the confession of sin restores our joy. That isn't going to happen until we start putting the blame where it belongs. It's so easy for us to try to blame other people for our own sin, for our own shortcomings, for our own lies, for our own transgressions, and for our own iniquities. What I love about David is that he didn't try to blame his sin on heredity: he didn't say, "It's my mama's fault; it's my daddy's fault; if my grandparents had been different...." He didn't blame it on society, either: he didn't say, "It's the environment that caused me to do what I did." David put the blame right where it belonged and took responsibility for his own sins. That serves as an example for us, because the only way we are going to be set free, the only way we are going to get our joy back, is when we stop blaming other people, heredity, or society and start taking responsibility for our own actions.

Look again at Psalm 51 and see how David took responsibility for his own sin:

- "Have mercy on *me*, O God, blot out *my* transgressions" (verse 1).
- "Wash away all *my* iniquity and cleanse *me* from *my* sin" (verse 2).

- "For I know *my* transgressions, and *my* sin is always before me" (verse 3).
- "Against you, you only, have *I* sinned" (verse 4).
- " Surely *I* was sinful at birth" (verse 5).
- "Cleanse *me* with hyssop, and I will be clean; wash *me*, and I will be whiter than snow" (verse 7).
- "Hide your face from *my* sins and blot out all *my* iniquity" (verse 9).
- "Create in *me* a pure heart, O God, and renew a steadfast spirit within *me*" (verse 10).
- "Restore to *me* the joy of your salvation and grant *me* a willing spirit, to sustain *me*" (verse 12).
- "Save *me* from bloodguilt, O God, the God who saves *me*" (verse 14).

Whenever we spell sin, we must spell it "s-**I**-n." We have to put the emphasis on the "I." It's not our mother's fault or our father's fault. It's not our husband, our wife, our former spouse, our ex-boyfriend or ex-girlfriend, and not our children who caused us to sin. Our boss didn't make us do this. And we can't even blame the devil because 1 Corinthians 10:13 tells us: "No temptation has seized you except what is common to man. And God is faithful; he will not let you be tempted beyond what you can bear. But when you are tempted, he will also provide a way out so that you can stand up under it." So if we fail to stand up to the temptation, it wasn't *God* who was unfaithful. It isn't until we acknowledge the sin in our own lives that we are able to be forgiven and have joy back in our lives.

Sin, Transgression and Iniquity

I noticed something else in the text. David employs three different words within verses 1 and 2 that most of us use interchangeably as though they were identical: blot out my *transgressions*; wash away all my *iniquity*; and cleanse me from my *sin*. While we *can* use these words interchangeably because they are all speaking of unrighteousness, the very fact that he uses all three in the same context indicates that each one carries a different connotation. *Transgression* is the noun form of the verb *to transgress*. "Trans" means to go across, or over, or beyond (a limit or boundary); "gress" relates to a command or law. Transgressions are often sins against another person because we fail to keep the commandment to "love your neighbor as yourself" (Matthew 22:39). *Sin*, on the other hand, is always committed against God. That's why David said, "Against you, you only, have I sinned." Even though he had *transgressed* against others, his *sin* was against God. *Iniquity* comes from *in*, meaning "not"; and *aequus*, meaning "just," "equal," or "righteous." So "iniquity" refers to that which is not just or righteous within me or inherent in my actions.

David is expressing the fact that we need to come to grips with all of these. Some of us want to go to God to ask for forgiveness, but we don't want to go back to the people we've hurt or against whom we've transgressed. We need to go and ask other folk to forgive us for what we've done to them. Jesus taught in Matthew 5:23-24: "If you are offering your gift at the altar and there remember that your brother has something against you, leave your gift there in front of the altar. First go and be reconciled to your brother; then come and offer your gift."

Iniquity is primarily that which we have to deal with on the inside. David goes from *confessing* sin to being cleansed *of* sin: "Cleanse me with hyssop, and I will be clean; wash me, and I will be whiter than snow" (v. 7). When I was a kid, we used to sing a song that asked, "What can wash away my sin?" and then offered the answer: "Nothing but the blood of Jesus." We would sing, "What can make me whole again?" and then respond, "Nothing but the blood of Jesus." God doesn't just want to forgive us, He wants to cleanse us. He wants to wash us and make us clean. It isn't enough for us to go to church every Sunday and keep asking God to forgive us for the same sins we brought to Him the week before—and the week before that. We have to get to the point where we confess our sins and believe that God has forgiven us our sins, but also know that He cleanses us from all unrighteousness. (See 1 John 1:9.)

Forgiveness is available to us; cleansing is available to us. That's what Calvary is all about; that's what the resurrection is all about. Jesus paid the penalty for your sin and mine. I don't have to walk around depressed, dismayed, disillusioned, and down; I can walk around with joy. Even though sin tries to steal my joy, God restores that joy when I confess that sin.

Remember that guilt brings us to repentance, but once we've asked God to forgive us, if we still feel guilty, that is not of God. Pastor Maurice Watson says that is "illegitimate guilt." If you've already asked God to forgive you of a sin and you are still feeling guilty about it, that's not God; that's the devil. Guilt is designed to bring you to repentance and when you repent of your sin, God forgives you, gives you another chance, and wipes the slate clean. So if you are still feeling guilty, that's a trick of the enemy to keep you from serving God because you are still dwelling on something that God has already forgiven.

Grace and Mercy

Most of us don't understand what we receive when we confess our sins. God gives us both grace and mercy. Grace is the unmerited favor of God. In other words, God blesses you and gives you something you don't deserve. Mercy, on the other hand, refers to God withholding from you what you do deserve. In short, something bad should have happened to you, but it didn't.

Let me give you some examples of mercy. You may have smoked enough weed and taken enough drugs that you should have become a drug addict. Others did drugs less than you and they're addicted while you are still free. It's not because you did the right thing; it's because the mercy of God withheld the addiction that should have been the natural consequence of your actions. You may have drunk enough alcohol that you should have become an alcoholic.

Others drank less than you did and today they cannot function in life because of their alcoholism, but you are still free. That's not because you didn't drink too much; it's because of the mercy of God. You may have slept casually with enough people that the odds are by now you should have come in contact with HIV/AIDS or contracted a sexually transmitted disease, yet you are in good health. That's because God's mercy withheld from you a serious consequence to which your behavior made you vulnerable.

Don't think that I am addressing you from a position of innocence—that I have always done the holy and righteous thing. I am human, just as you are, and I have sinned, just as you have. The only reason I am a preacher of the gospel today, and the only reason I have joy in my life today, is because of God's grace and mercy. God's grace brought me forgiveness, and His mercy kept me from experiencing what I deserved. There are things that should have happened to me, but they didn't because of the mercy of God.

Right now, you may be feeling down and depressed because of some sin you have committed. What I'm trying to tell you is that if you ask for mercy, mercy will show up in your situation. You may protest, "But you don't know what I've done. You don't know where I've been. You don't know the mistakes I've made." No, I don't, but I do know the mercy of God. The Bible says that God's mercy is like an ocean; that's how great the mercy of God is.

Once when I was flying across the ocean, I looked out and God spoke to me. He told me that His mercy is like this ocean. I looked down, and as far as I could see from the east to the west to the north and to the south, all I could see was ocean. There was nothing but water. God said, "Jeffrey Johnson, that's how great My mercy is. There is no mistake that you've made, nothing you've done wrong, that My mercy cannot cover. Then the Holy Spirit said, "And, Jeffrey Johnson, you are only looking at the top of the ocean. You don't know how deep it runs!" Most of us don't know how deep the mercy of God runs.

Mercy and Justice

I'll never forget hearing Donald Parsons, pastor of Logos Baptist Assembly in Chicago, share this illustration about Mercy and Justice once scheduling a meeting for the next day at noon. They were going to discuss humanity and what to do with humanity's sin. Of course, Justice wanted us to get just what we deserved: "The wages of sin is death." Mercy, however, wanted to set us free because "the gift of God is eternal life" (Romans 6:23).

At twelve noon, of course, Justice showed up for the meeting on time, but Mercy was late. One o'clock came, and Mercy still had not shown up. Four o'clock: no Mercy. Six o'clock: no Mercy. Now the sun was going down, but still no Mercy. As Justice is getting ready to leave, he looks into the distance and sees what might be Mercy. But then he thinks it can't be Mercy because the figure coming toward him is wearing clothes that are dripping wet, covered in soot, and ripped and torn. As the figure got closer, Justice could see that there were holes in his hands and holes in his feet. "That can't be Mercy," Justice thought.

But then Mercy came close enough that Justice could identify him. He said, "Mercy, you are late for our meeting. Where have you been?" Mercy responded, "I know I should have been here on time, but I had some things I had to do." Justice asked inquisitively, "Well, what happened to you? Why are your clothes all wet, dirty, and torn?" Mercy replied, "I would have been on time, but as I was passing by the Red Sea, I heard Moses cry out, 'Lord, have mercy!' And so, I had to stop and hold back the waters of the Red Sea so that the children of Israel could cross on dry ground. That's why I'm soaking wet."

Mercy continued, "I still could have made it on time, but as I passed through Babylon, I heard Shadrach, Meshach, and Abednego calling out, 'Lord, have mercy!' So I had to stop and get in the fire with them to protect them. That's why my clothes are covered with soot and smoke." He went on, "I still could have made it only slightly late, but as I was leaving Babylon, I heard Daniel say, 'Lord, have mercy!' So I had to close the mouths of the lions so that Daniel could spend the night in the lion's den and come out all right. That's why my clothes are ripped and torn."

Then he said, "And I still could have gotten here earlier, but as I went on and passed through Jerusalem, I heard a thief on a cross cry out, 'Lord, have mercy!' So I had to take the thief from the cross and accompany him to Paradise. That's why I've got holes in my hands and holes in my feet." Then Mercy said abruptly, "I'm sorry I was late, but I can't even stay here right now, because somebody who was reading a book just set it down and suddenly called out, 'Lord, have mercy!' I've got to go." My friend, whatever you've done, whatever mistakes you've made, just call on God. He will have mercy.

David said to God, "Restore unto me the *joy* of your salvation" (v. 12). Notice he didn't say, "Restore unto me *salvation*." He didn't lose his salvation when he committed adultery. He didn't lose salvation when he committed murder. What he lost was the joy associated with salvation. When you put your faith in Jesus Christ, God becomes your Father, and He is always going to be your Father. That's why when you pray, you address Him as "Our Father." The Spirit of Jesus, God's Son, resides in our hearts and cries out from our lips, "Abba, Father."

When you sin, you don't lose your *relationship* with God, but you mess up your *fellowship* with God. Remember when you did something wrong during your childhood? If you messed up by disobeying your parents, your mother didn't stop being your mother, and your father didn't quit being your father. The relationship was still intact, but the fellowship was messed up. If you have sinned and feel distant from God right now, you need to understand that you didn't lose your relationship with God; you messed up your fellowship with God. But I dare you to say, "Lord, have mercy!"

Giving, Praising, Witnessing

God restores to us the joy of salvation. So what do we do when we get our joy back? It tells us in verse 13: "Then I will teach transgressors your ways, and sinners will turn back to you." So whenever you get your joy back, it's time for you to start teaching other folk God's way. Verse 15 says, "O Lord, open my lips, and my mouth will declare your praise." Whenever your joy is restored, you've got to start praising—God's way. The last verse says, "Then there will be righteous sacrifices, whole burnt offerings to delight you; then bulls will be offered on your altar." Whenever you get your joy back, you've got to start giving—God's way. When you get your joy back, it isn't just so you can go to church and have a good time. When you get your joy back, you've got to start teaching sinners God's way.

You see, most folk think that when you give, somehow God is trying to take something from you. On the contrary! When you give, God isn't trying to take something from you; God is trying to give something *to* you. Mel Gibson found out when he felt compelled to produce *The Passion of the Christ* that no one shared his passion for making the movie. No one thought a movie about Jesus could be worth all that much. When potential backers refused to participate, Gibson reportedly invested $50 million of his own money in its production and marketing. He felt that he had to introduce the passion of Christ, the story of Jesus' death on the cross for the sins of the world, into a secular society that didn't grasp the real meaning of Jesus' sacrifice. In the process of following his vision, Gibson learned that we can't beat God giving. His movie earned over $600 million worldwide.

That's my word to anybody who might be stingy with God. That person needs to know that whenever you offer money to God, you don't lose it. Whenever you give to God, God will give it back to you, "good measure, pressed down, shaken together and running over" (Luke 6:38).

Whenever you get your joy back, you need to start giving, start telling others about God's way, and you need to start praising God. I don't understand some folk who claim to have experienced the mercy of God, who claim to have their sins forgiven, and who claim to have joy, but they never praise God. Verse 15 says, in essence, "God, if You open my mouth, I am going to give You praise." Too many of us are too quiet when it comes to God. We say, "Well, I can praise God in my own way," but nowhere in the Bible does it tell you to praise God in your own way. God always tells us how to praise Him: "O clap your hands, all ye people" (Psalm 47:1 KJV). He always tells us how to praise Him: "Come, let us bow down in worship, let us kneel before the Lord our Maker" (Psalm 95:6). He always tells us how to praise Him: "Make a joyful noise" (Psalm 100:1 KJV), and "Praise him with tambourine and dancing" (Psalm 150:4). When I go into the house of God, I don't go in to do things my way; I go in to do things God's way. Then, when folk look at me, they can tell I'm on the winning team. It isn't because of what I drive, what I own, or where I live. It's because I've got joy.

In basketball, if a player hits a three-pointer, everyone begins to shout. In baseball, if your team hits a home run, everybody begins to shout. In football, if you score a touchdown, everybody begins to shout. In Christianity, if God has hit a home run for you, has hit a three-pointer for you, or has scored a touchdown for you, somebody ought to give Him praise. If God has ever done anything for you, you ought to give God some praise.

Rev. Solomon Kinloch, Jr., pastor of Triumph Church in Detroit, offers this illustration: Let's pretend that we're in a court of law. I want to swear you in as a witness. Raise your right hand and repeat after me: I swear to tell the truth, the whole truth, and nothing but the truth. Now state your name for the court. Now I want to ask you some questions, and I want to remind you that you've been sworn in. If you tell a lie, that's perjury, and it will put you in bondage. So let me ask you some questions:

Has God ever made a way for you?

Has God ever done something for you that you couldn't do for yourself?

Has God ever healed your body?

Has God ever opened a door for you that you couldn't open for yourself?

(Please speak up so that the court can hear you.)

Has God ever made a way out of no way?

Won't God give you joy?

Has mercy ever made a way for you?

If you answered yes to any of these questions, you need to be telling others about God, praising God, and giving to God. He is worthy to be praised and trusted.

VIII

The Greatest
Comeback Ever

[19]On the evening of that first day of the week, when
the disciples were together, with the doors locked for
fear of the Jews, Jesus came and stood among them
and said, "Peace be with you!" [20]After he said this, he
showed them his hands and side. The disciples were
overjoyed when they saw the Lord.

(John 20:19-20)

Lindsey Boyd, a young Indiana University
student, was critically injured in a car crash in
the southern part of Indiana. Her car flipped over
several times, leaving her unconscious, paralyzed,
and with a big gash in her head. She had to be life-
lined from the roadside where she had the accident to
Wishard Memorial Hospital to be treated. She was so
bad off that one news account said she had died, but
that she was only being kept on life support, waiting

for her family to show up to say their last good-byes. In actual fact, however, she had surgery, and the doctors were able to relieve pressure which allowed her to move again. They treated her head injury, along with the large gash that she had received. It took a long time and some therapy, but now she is walking, enrolled in school again, and is doing fine. She is still committed to Christ.

We serve a God who is an expert in comebacks. Even though people have reported that you are finished, that it's over, that there's nothing more that can be done, that you are simply holding on until the end, I would encourage you to put your life in God's hands. He is the greatest doctor ever. He is able to perform surgery, relieve pressure, apply a healing touch, and get you back on your feet again.

A Risen Savior

The Bible shows us how great God is in terms of comebacks by telling us about the resurrection of Jesus. The resurrection is perhaps the most important belief in Christendom because without the resurrection, there is no salvation; there is no redemption, and there is no regeneration. "If Christ be not raised.... we are of all men most miserable" (1 Corinthians 15:17, 19 KJV). But Jesus is risen. He is alive forevermore. It is this belief in the resurrection that causes us to become the children of God. Indeed, we need to believe in all aspects of Christ's life, but believing that Jesus turned water into wine, that He fed a multitude with a few fish and small loaves of bread, or that He walked on water does not in itself save us. It is only by believing that Christ died for our sins and rose again that we find salvation. It doesn't matter what sin we've committed or how messed up our lives are, the apostle Paul tells us, "If you confess with your mouth, 'Jesus is Lord,' and believe in your heart that God raised him from the dead, you will be saved" (Romans 10:9).

The only way to be saved and get right with God is to believe in the death, burial, and resurrection of Christ. Jesus died on Friday, and God raised Him three days later. I know we talk about how Jesus "got up," but the Bible doesn't say, "Jesus got up." It says that God raised Him. This indicates to us that God can step into our hopeless, dead situations and raise us up out of them. When God raised Jesus from the dead, Mary Magdalene was one of the first people to show up at the tomb. I love that because this is the same woman who had seven devils possessing her, which shows us that it doesn't matter how many devils we've hung with in the past: if we connect with Jesus, He will give us new life. Mary Magdalene was given the opportunity to see Jesus resurrected. Later, Jesus walked with two men on the road to Emmaus for seven and a half miles, but it wasn't until He broke bread with them that they realized this was the resurrected Christ.

Then Jesus showed up in John 20:19 in His resurrected body. The disciples were hiding out in a house "for fear of the Jews." They believed that the same people who arrested and crucified Jesus would be coming after them next, so they were afraid and in hiding. The text says it is in the evening; it is in the midst of darkness, in the midst of their difficulty; they are in a devastating situation. They had believed Jesus was the Christ until He died, and now they think it is all over. The hope for the kingdom is gone. There is nothing left now, and they are in their darkest hour. It was in that very moment that the text says, "Jesus came and stood among them." Jesus has a way of showing up in our darkness. When we don't know which way to turn or which way to go, when we are facing devastation and difficulty, it is then that Jesus shows up. And His presence makes a difference in the midst of our problems.

Jesus Unlocks Doors

Furthermore, Jesus even showed up on the inside of a room with locked doors. The disciples were so afraid that they had locked themselves in and other folk out. But here comes Jesus, showing up on the inside of that locked door. That's why locked doors don't bother me anymore. Grandma says that when doors have been closed in your face, God can open doors that no man can close. If you connect with Jesus, He can show up even if you are locked up, locked in, or locked out. He is the Master with the master key. Maybe you've been locked out of a job or some career opportunity, or some door to education has been shut in your face. Perhaps you have been locked out of some promotion because of sexism, racism, ageism, or some other bias. But I want you to know that God is Someone who can get on the other side of locked doors. I promise He can open doors that have been shut in your face. He is able to give you a comeback.

One day, I pulled up to my house and pushed the button to open my garage door, but it didn't open. It had been opening just fine for years, but now, all of a sudden, it wouldn't open for me. When I looked it over, I discovered that the reason the door wouldn't open, even though I was pushing the right button, was because the sensors had gotten out of line. There are sensors on either side of the garage door, and as long as they are lined up and I'm pushing the right button, the door always opens. This time, however, I was pushing the right button, but the door wasn't opening. I didn't know how the sensors got out of line, but I got down on my knees and got them lined back up. Then, when I pushed the button, the door opened. Let me tell you why doors may have remained closed to you, even though you may have been pushing all the right buttons. It could be that your life is out of line with Jesus. If you get on your knees and line your life up with Jesus, you will discover that God can open doors nobody can close.

God's Presence Makes the Difference

It was Jesus' presence which made a difference in the lives of the believers in that room. When He entered on the other side of the locked door, the text says the disciples were glad. Why were they glad? Nothing had changed. They still were in the dark. They were still in the same difficult and devastating situation. The Jews were still looking for them, so their lives were in danger. Nothing about their situation or location had changed. But what had changed was their disposition because of the presence of God. The text says they became glad, not because the situation had changed, but because the presence of Jesus showed up in their darkness. Even today, if we could sit down and talk together, you might tell me about a situation that has you angry, depressed, or frightened. Or you may tell me about a location you are in right now where nothing is working out for you. But sometimes, God wants to change our disposition before He changes our situation. Sometimes He wants us to get excited about the fact that He is still present with us. And when we know who He is, we will be glad instead of being sad. It is God's presence that makes the difference.

I'm really proud of my son J. Allen, who is a student at Payne College in Augusta, Georgia. He taught me something a long time ago. When Jay was a little boy, he was afraid of the dark. We had talked about it several times. Here I was, telling a little boy, "You don't have to be afraid of the dark, because whether the light is on or off, the room is the same. There is nothing different just because the light goes out." Jay responded, "Daddy, I'm still afraid of the dark." At times, Jay would go to bed in *his* room; but when he woke up in the morning, he was in *my* room. So I said, "Jay, you can't do that. You can't sleep between your mom and me; that just isn't going to work. When you go to sleep in your bed, you stay in your bed." Then I asked again, "Why do you keep coming into our room?" He replied again, "Daddy, you know I'm afraid of the dark." I said, "Yes, I understand that you're afraid of the dark, but it's dark in our room, too. In fact, it is darker in our room than it is in your room." Then Jay helped to reveal a theological understanding I have never forgotten. He said, "But, Daddy, you are in here." Think about it. Jay woke up in a dark room, walked down a dark hall, walked into another dark room, and went fast asleep. He was saying, "Even though it's dark, I am not afraid, because my father is present with me." I hope you can grasp that thought. Yes, in your current situation, it is difficult, it is dark, and it is scary. Yet, as long as God your Father is with you, you don't have to be afraid.

Jesus' words to His disciples were, "Peace be with you!" He hadn't changed their situation or location, but He had given them peace. Remember that the peace of God surpasses all human understanding. God will guard your heart and mind if you keep your mind stayed on Jesus. (See Philippians 4:7.) He will give you peace in the midst of your difficulty and peace in the midst of your sorrow. All hell can be breaking loose around you, but Jesus can come in and give you peace.

Scars Tell a Story

Watch this. After giving them peace, He also showed them His hands and His side. The text says the disciples were overjoyed. You would think that if Jesus showed them His hands with the nail prints, and the hole in His side, it would scare them because the same people who did that to Him were still out looking for them. But no, they were overjoyed. That's because even the disciples knew that scars tell stories. The story that these scars were telling is that no matter what your enemy has done to you, you can still come back from that experience.

Romans 8:11 says that the same Spirit that raised Jesus from the dead is now in you. You've invited Christ into your life, so His Holy Spirit lives inside of you. That's the same Spirit that raised Christ from the dead. Do you understand what Jesus came back from? He had a friend who denied Him three times; another friend betrayed Him by kissing Him; the very people He helped falsely accused Him; the religious community turned on Him; the Roman soldiers, who were people from another culture, helped attack Him; He was whipped with leather straps that had glass and metal embedded in them so it tore the flesh from His body; He was laid on a cross and had spikes pounded into His hands and His feet; His cross was raised and He died between two thieves; a spear was thrust into His side; He was buried in another man's tomb; a stone was rolled in front of the tomb; a seal was put on the stone and a guard placed in front of the tomb. Jesus went through all of that, but on the morning of the third day, after all the hell He had been through, God stepped into the situation and raised Jesus from the dead. So Paul assures us that whatever hell we're going through now, God has placed the same Spirit within us that raised Jesus from the dead. Jesus showed the disciples His scars because scars tell stories.

You undoubtedly have some kind of scar in *your* life. It may not be physical, because not all scars are physical. Some scars *are* physical, but some are emotional and others psychological. Every scar tells a story. Every scar reminds you of some event you went through that gave it to you. Many of us need to understand that the deeper the scar, the worse the scar, the greater the memory. Some of us are trying to forget what we've gone through, but the scar is so deep that we can't forget. Most of us would prefer to get only scratches in the kingdom because they heal quickly and we can forget about them easily. But a scar tells the story of an event that sometimes we wish had never happened, yet we can't forget about it because of the scar that we have. But the very fact that we are still here is a testimony to the fact that God has kept us, even in the midst of the difficulty. Yes, we've got scars; yes, we've been deeply cut; yes, we wish we could forget, but we can't. But the fact that we're still here is an indication that God is in the comeback business.

Here's an important lesson for us as followers of Christ. Unless we get bruised, we cannot be used. Some of us want to be used by God, but we don't want to be bruised by God. When Jesus went through the crucifixion, He said, "Nobody *took* My life." Some people today are still arguing over whether it was the Jews or the Romans who were most responsible for the crucifixion. But Jesus said, "Nobody took My life; I laid it down. And because I laid it down, I can pick it up again." And the scars that Jesus showed them let them know what He was able to come back from. When people had done their worst to Him, He rose again. Don't give up on God. He is in the comeback business.

Purpose in the Pain

There was a purpose in the crucifixion. And there is a purpose in your trials and sorrows as well. Everything God has allowed you to go through is for a reason. Even though you have been scarred, when you come back from what you've gone through, you can show people your scars. You can show somebody your side. God wants you to let somebody else know what you've been through because that person may be going through the same thing, and your story— your testimony—can bring that person comfort. But had you not been bruised, how could you ever be used? How can you tell somebody that God is Bread in a starving land if you've never been hungry? How can you tell somebody that God is a Friend to the friendless if you've never had a friend stab you in the back? How can you tell somebody that God is a Mother to the motherless and a Father to the fatherless if your parents have always been there for you? How are you going to tell somebody that God is a Doctor who has never lost a patient if you have never been sick? How can you tell somebody that God is a Lawyer who has never lost a case if you've never been in trouble? But if you've been bruised, you can be used. The very fact that you are still here is an indication that God is in the comeback business. When Jesus showed the disciples His scars, He was telling them, "Yes, I was wounded, but I still won." Do you know what it means to be wounded, but still have the victory?

There was a disciple who was missing when Jesus appeared to them behind the locked door on that day. Judas, of course, had already killed himself, but there was still another one missing. Thomas was not there. The disciples were so excited, they told him later, "We have seen the Lord!" But Thomas said he was not going to believe it until he could see the nail prints in the Lord's hands, put his fingers over the place where the nails were, and put his hand into Jesus' side where the spear had pierced Him. So, the next time the disciples were together, Jesus showed up again. He already knew the doubts that were in Thomas's mind, so Jesus came in and told Thomas, "Put your fingers in the holes in my hand; put your hand in the hole in my side." Thomas didn't have to touch Jesus. Once he saw Him, he cried out, "My Lord and my God!" When you begin to see the Lord by faith, when you understand the power of the resurrection, you, too, cry out to Jesus, "My Lord and my God!" Do you understand now why the resurrection is so important and why you have to believe in the resurrection? When you know that God raised Him, you know Him as Lord and God.

God Is In Control

Remember that in verse 20, the disciples got overjoyed "when they saw the Lord." Notice that it doesn't say, "when they saw Jesus." Had it said "Jesus," it would have been referencing the salvation that is offered through Jesus: "Call his name Jesus: for he shall save his people from their sins" (Matthew 1:21 KJV). But verse 20 says specifically, "when they saw the *Lord*," because it is making reference to His sovereignty. The Greek word for *Lord* is *kurios*. It means master, owner, the one who has decision-making power. When they saw not Jesus, but the Lord, the One in charge, they were overjoyed. Now, you may be saying, "But I thought Jesus *was* the Lord." Yes! That's what I'm trying to tell you. Jesus is the Lord: the One who saves you is the One who can keep you. He is still in charge. Your boss is not in charge of your life. Neither is your ex-wife, your ex-husband, or your enemy. GOD is still in charge. He's in the comeback business.

I heard a story about nine climbers who headed up Mt. Hood in Oregon, one of them being just fourteen years old. They got to a certain height, and all of a sudden, five of them began to slip and fall. When they began to slide down this mountain, the ice and snow came down on top of them, totally covering them up. Three of those who fell died, but two survived after being rescued by a Black Hawk helicopter. Of the two who survived, one of them was the fourteen-year-old boy. When the media interviewed him after the rescue, they asked him if he was afraid.

He said, "Yes, I was afraid, because I fell." "Were you totally covered up?" the reporters asked. "Yes, I was totally covered up with ice and snow." "Did you cry?" "Yes, I cried. I couldn't see anything. I had fallen. I was totally covered up. I was afraid." "Was there ever a point that you thought you would not be rescued?" He replied, "No, I always knew I was going to be rescued." "How did you know that? You fell, you were totally covered up, and three others didn't even make it. You cried and you were afraid, but you never thought there was a time that you wouldn't make it?" He affirmed, "No, I always knew I was going to be rescued. I knew that because before we started to climb up the mountain, my father tied a rope around me that was connected to a rope around him. So I knew that as long as my father was okay, I would be okay. Even though it looked dark and seemed really bad, I knew that my father would pull me out." He got out of his situation because of his connection with his father.

We need to know that as travelers through this life, we *will* fall on hard times, we *will* fall on difficulties, and we *will* fall on trials and tragedies. But as long as we're connected to our Father, we can trust Him to pull us out. No matter how bad it seems, God has not fallen, and He will not let go of the bond that connects us to Him. He *will* come to our rescue by pulling us out of that difficult situation.

Sent to Serve

After giving them peace, Jesus told His disciples: "As my Father sent me, I am sending you" (v. 21). He is giving them purpose. Why do you think God would bring you through all He has brought you through if He did not have a purpose, or have anything for you to do? In effect, Jesus said to His disciples that it was never His intention for them to sit in a house behind locked doors, and do nothing. It was never His intention for them to lock disciples in and sinners out. He told them He had a purpose for them: "As my Father sent me, I am sending you." Now, most of what Jesus did was not done inside a temple; most of what He did was done outside. So, if Jesus is sending us like the Father had sent Him, He isn't expecting us just to go to church, and to sit and do nothing. I think what He's saying is that we have to get outside and serve.

Church is not just a place to go to sing, shout, and sit and listen to a sermon. It's a place where you are supposed to get informed and inspired so that you can go out and serve God beyond the walls of the church. Now, I know why some of us are not serving, why some of us are content just to come and sit in church. It's the same reason that the ten disciples in John 20 sat: it was because they thought it was over. Jesus had died on the cross, and they had buried Him. They had rolled a stone in front of the tomb and put a seal on the stone, and there were guards stationed in front of the tomb. They thought it was all over. So they went into the house and sat and did nothing. That's why some of us come into the house of God and sit and do nothing—because we think it's over. We think life is over. We had a bad marriage, so we think life is over. We lost our job, so we think life is over. We never got the level of education we needed, so we think life is over. We're dealing with some bad sickness or disease, so we think life is over. That's why we come and sit and do nothing.

But let me tell you, it's not over till *God* says it's over! That's why Jesus showed up: to tell the disciples to get out of there and start serving. He had to tell them it wasn't over! And I'm trying to tell you that it isn't over. You need to know that so that instead of sitting down and doing nothing, you will get up and go fulfill God's purpose for your life.

Don't Give Up!

In January 2007, during the AFC Championship game between the Indianapolis Colts and the New England Patriots, somebody invited me to the game. I was sitting at the 50-yard line in one of the suites. This was a major hook-up! When I went into the suite, someone told me, "Pastor, you just eat whatever you want; whatever you want, it's yours." So, I was eating and relaxing, watching this amazing game from a suite on the 50-yard line, seeing Coach Tony Dungy lead the Indianapolis Colts to victory in the AFC Championship title game against Tom Brady with his three Super Bowl wins and his two Super Bowl MVP awards. But by halftime, we were losing by the score of 21-3. I couldn't stand to see Tony Dungy's face, the way he was looking on the sidelines. And I've got friends on this team, so I thought, *I can't take this! This thing is over; it's done.* I wanted to leave because I thought it was over, and I didn't want to watch it play out the way I knew it was going to. But then, I couldn't just go in, eat, and leave at halftime because it would look as though I weren't grateful for the hook-up. So I stayed, not because I had hope for the team, but so I wouldn't offend the one who gave me the opportunity to be there.

So there we were at halftime, down 21-3. But in the second half, the Colts scored 35 points to win the game 38-34 against three-time Super Bowl champs, the New England Patriots. Here's what I'm trying to tell you. This was the greatest comeback in AFC Championship title history, and I almost missed it because I thought it was over before it was over! My friend, before you walk out on God, before you turn your back on Jesus, you need to realize that the very fact you are still alive is an indication that it isn't over. God's got a second half! He will give you a comeback!

Power for His Purpose

The text says that Jesus breathed on His disciples. He gave them His power by breathing on them. One thing I love about God is that He never gives you purpose without giving you power to live out the purpose. The purpose is what He wants you to do; the power is how He wants you to do it. What Jesus did was to breathe on His disciples. And as He did that, He said, "Receive the Holy Spirit." What you don't want to do is to try to deal with your difficulty, darkness, and devastation without the power of God's Holy Spirit. It's almost like Jesus came to His disciples and said, "I'm going to send you the way the Father sent Me." I can imagine the disciples, in their excitement, getting ready to rush out the door, but Jesus called them back: "Where are you going?" "Well, Jesus," they replied, "You said that You were going to send us the way the Father sent you, so we're going to serve." But Jesus says, "I wouldn't try to deal with everything on the other side of that door without the Holy Spirit, if I were you."

I think Jesus is saying the same thing even to those who are reading this book. As you've been reading, you may feel inspired. You may know now that, even though you thought your life was over, it isn't over yet. You may now realize that God has more in store for you than simply sitting in a church building once a week and doing nothing. You may be excited because you sense a fresh purpose for your life, and you are eager to see what God has in store for you. But Jesus is saying, "Wait a minute. Don't go out until you have received the Holy Spirit. Don't try to go back to that messed-up job without the Holy Spirit. Don't go back to that failing marriage without the Holy Spirit. Don't go back to face the demands of corporate America without the Holy Spirit."

You don't have to face your darkness and difficulties alone. God will breathe on you and give you His Holy Spirit. But now, for God to breathe on you, that means you have to be close to Him. Some folk never operate in the Spirit of God because they don't get close enough to Him.

We have to stop going to church late, leaving early, showing up once a month, and thinking we've got this thing covered. We don't have it covered if we're distant from God. We must first learn to pray and fast, then give and live. When we get close to Jesus, He breathes on us and the Holy Spirit fills us. I thank God for every victory I have, but I have to give all the credit to God. I thank God for every door that's been opened, every way that's been made, every dollar I've received, and every degree that I have, because if it had not been for God breathing on me, I would not have made it.

In my office right now, I have a steamer that I use to straighten my clothes out because sometimes, even though they are clean, they may have become wrinkled. So when I need to, I press my clothes with a steamer so that I can look presentable. The steamer has a container that holds about a gallon of water that has to be filled up. Then there's a heating apparatus that connects to the water and when it's turned on, the heat touches the water. When the water gets hot enough, the steam runs up a handle, and I can use it to straighten my clothes without much effort or energy. I have used this steamer a lot, and it really comes in handy.

But one day, I wasn't getting the steam that I usually get. I was putting forth a lot of energy and effort, but I could barely tell a difference in my clothes. Later on, I was in my office, and I decided to check out the steamer. Instead of filling it with "just enough" water, I filled that container up. When I filled it up, you should have seen all the steam that came pouring out! Earlier, I had to put forth so much strength and energy because I was trying to do the work without having the container filled. Some of us may even now be trying to straighten out something in our lives. We're working so hard and putting forth so much effort, but nothing is happening, and we can't see any difference. But if we get close enough to God to let Him breathe upon us, He will fill us with His Holy Spirit and empower us to straighten out the situations in our lives.

When Jesus was preparing to go back to the Father, He promised His disciples that He wouldn't leave them alone; He would give them a Comforter. The Holy Spirit is that Promised One—the One who continues to teach us, guide us, comfort us, and empower us. He is the same Spirit who raised Christ from the dead, and He lives within those of us who have embraced Christ as our personal Savior.

God desires for us to make a comeback from whatever is our own dead situation. God wants us to get our lives back. Put your life in God's hands, and allow Him to work within you and through you. Make a commitment today not to give up until you achieve your victory.

Printed in the United States
130242LV00002BB/1/P